RADICAL RULES FOR SCHOOLS:

ADAPTIVE ACTION FOR COMPLEX CHANGE

LESLIE PATTERSON

ROYCE HOLLADAY

GLENDA H. EOYANG

HUMAN
SYSTEMS
DYNAMICS
Institute

ISBN-13: 978-0615766263

Human Systems Dynamics Institute

50 East Golden Lake Road

Circle Pines, MN 55014

www.hsdinstitute.org

To Mother/Buddy/Ruth,

who set the conditions for this work.

Acknowledgements

In complex systems, we know that the whole is different from the sum of the parts. That is clearly true for the whole of what we have learned about the power of simple rules to enhance adaptive capacity in schools. We are profoundly grateful to our friends and colleagues who have contributed to Human Systems Dynamics over the years, particularly as it informs our work in schools. As with any long-term inquiry project, there are too many individuals to name, but we thank the self-organizing networks of colleagues we have had the pleasure and honor of working with as this book has emerged.

First, the Human Systems Dynamics Associate's Network has supported our work individually and collectively. What a vital network of teacher and learners that has been for us over the years.

We also express a special thanks to all the professionals in the New Haven Unified School District who joined us in our collaborative initiative during the 2011-12 school year. Superintendent Kari McVeigh and the Chief Academic Officer Wendy Gudalewicz have been particularly engaging and insightful colleagues in this work. Many of the stories and quotes from educators in this book are based on interviews with these amazing professionals.

We also thank our good colleagues with The Ball Foundation Education Initiatives--Bob Hill, Barbara Iversen, Michael Palmisano, and Rex Babiera. Their support and collaboration were central to the work in NHUSD and to our learning in the last two years.

Lynne Krehbeil, Sara Mullett, Jim Johnson, and Mark Sander have, through their work with Minneapolis Public Schools, helped explore and expand applications of HSD in creating student-centered services for learners. Bertina Combes, Educational Psychology faculty member at University of North Texas, invited us to use these concepts in a doctoral program for leaders in Special Education. We are also grateful to the many other teachers, students, administrators, board members, and parents who have allowed us the privilege of working in their schools and districts as we learn with them about the dynamics of human systems. Many of the examples and stories in this book come from our work with those impressive and committed teachers and learners.

We say another thanks to the teacher consultants in the North Star of Texas Writing Project, a National Writing Project Site, for their thoughtful responses to this work. We especially thank Carol Wickstrom, the Director of that site and a faculty member in the College of Education at University of North Texas--an amazing teacher and colleague who has helped us see the potential for these simple rules.

And we say a final thank you to our families -- who challenge us to follow these simple, yet radical, rules by day.

An Introductory Note

School reform in the United States continues to disappoint. Critics point to persistent achievement gaps and drop-out rates, especially among students from poverty and students of color. The blame usually falls on educators in general and teachers in particular. In turn, many educators blame the oppressive emphasis on high stakes testing and the unintended consequences of federal mandates. To be fair, school reform in the U.S has been a long-term proposition, dating back to the 19th century. Since the mid-1980s, the most recent wave of reform, we have seen significant success at specific sites for relatively short periods of time, but those successes have not spread, nor have they sustained. No one is happy.

Admittedly, the challenges are overwhelming. The systems are huge and highly diverse; the results are unpredictable and difficult to document; and political and interpersonal relationships inside and outside classrooms are massively entangled. Large numbers of highly diverse, interdependent individuals, groups, and communities bring diverse agendas, histories, and cultures. The challenge is to build structures that sustain teaching and learning within this complexity—structures to help us navigate this turbulent and shifting landscape.

In such systems, it will never be enough to focus only on the most urgent challenges. Most of these urgent issues are merely symptoms of dysfunctional dynamics deep within the system. They emerge as a result of the complex dynamics of human thought and interaction, and to work on only those individual issues is to ignore the underlying conditions that trigger and exacerbate those symptoms. It's like treating arthritis with aspirin—it relieves some of the pain, but does not address the underlying disease—and the treatment can even trigger other problems and unintended consequences. The more we can learn about the underlying dynamics of these complex systems, the better we can work from the inside to trigger and sustain significant transformation. In fact, it is our belief that this kind of dramatic transformation is only possible from the inside.

Such transformation is not magic. Complexity scientists call it **"self-organization."** We believe it is possible to explain the dynamics of self-organization and use that understanding to help everyone in the system adapt to changes within and outside the system. Our goal is to build **adaptive capacity** throughout the system. The more adaptive capacity we have, both individually and collectively, the more responsive, productive, and joyful we can be. The purpose of this book is to explore how to build adaptive capacity by helping people see, understand, and influence the patterns of interaction and decision-making in their work.

This is meant to be a practical book. We recommend a short set of simple (yet radical) rules to build adaptive capacity in classrooms, schools, and the larger system. We argue that, when the people in a complex school system function according to a shared set of rules, their actions will trigger system wide transformation. The particular rules we recommend are grounded in Glenda Eoyang's work on human systems dynamics (HSD) and her extensive experience as the Executive Director of the Human Systems Dynamics Institute, with a wide range of organizations around the world (see http://www.hsdinstitute.org).

We argue that, if educators consistently follow these simple rules, the underlying dynamics of teaching and learning will shift, and the system will self-organize to become ever more sensitive, responsive, and robust. No one can predict the precise direction, speed, or nature of those changes, but the interactions in schools will begin to reflect the adaptability and responsiveness inherent in these seven simple rules. This willingness and ability to respond to the unexpected is what we mean by **adaptive capacity**.

We recognize that this may sound simplistic, almost like magical thinking. How can a mere set of simple rules transform the massive educational bureaucracy that we call school? But self-organization in complex adaptive systems is a powerful force. (In fact, the unwieldy and unresponsive bureaucracy we see today has resulted from decades of self-organizing dynamics.) Our challenge is to see, understand, utilize, and influence the powerful self-organizing dynamics in the systems where we live and work.

Anyone familiar with recent research and practice related to school reform will notice similarities with other work on school leadership, instruction, and reform—Fullan, Hargreaves, Marshall, Darling-Hammond, Schlechty, Ravitch, Marzano, and many others. These and other reformers are cited throughout the book. Their work points to seven critical challenges for school reformers:

- **engagement** (especially among students)
- **sustainability** (of systems improvement and student learning gains)
- **focus** (on what really matters)
- **collaboration** (among all stakeholders)
- **coherence** (across instructional and administrative approaches)
- **risk-taking** (inherent in taking an inquiry stance)
- **joyful practice** (among all stakeholders)

Each of the simple rules we recommend in this book addresses one of these challenges. For each rule, we also recommend one or more methods and/or models to help readers implement the rule. Some of these will be familiar to educators; others are unique to human systems dynamics (HSD). We identify these practices as "models" because they help us think about our work differently and "methods" because they provide concrete tools to help us do the work.

The following table provides an overview of the simple rules and these methods/models.

Table 0.1: Introductory overview of simple rules and methods.

SIMPLE RULE	EXPLANATION	METHOD/ MODEL
Teach and learn in every interaction.	Teaching and learning are our central business and passion, and, therefore, a logical and powerful place to begin this discussion of simple rules. In complex systems, teaching and learning for everyone make for an adaptive system. Adaptive (or generative) teaching and learning invite enthusiastic **engagement**, which is certainly an issue that reformers see as critical. A major challenge for educators is to engage learners (of all ages) in authentic teaching and learning.	Simple Rules Complex Adaptive System (CAS) Adaptive Action
Pay attention to patterns in the whole, part, and greater whole.	From a human systems dynamics perspective, teaching and learning are about emergent patterns throughout the system. To understand how to work in these systems, we need to understand how patterns emerge across each scale in each system—in their parts and in the greater whole. Understanding and working with these emerging realities mean that we can take action toward **sustainability** of the generative patterns we want to see in system.	Coherence Constraints Fractals/ Scaling
See, understand, and influence patterns.	Once we understand how patterns emerge in complex adaptive systems, we can **focus** on what matters. We can focus on the patterns we want to see and the actions we can take to enhance those patterns across the system. This helps us avoid the fragmentation that characterizes most bureaucracies.	Conditions for Self-Organization (CDE) Constraints
Recognize and build on assets of self and others.	No one works in isolation in a school system. From a human systems dynamics perspective, it is critical to build **collaboration** among all stakeholders. In collaborative work, we build on everyone's strengths. That helps us build adaptive capacity in ourselves and in others throughout the system.	Generative Engagement Coupling Conflict Circles
Seek the true and the useful.	Historically, educational ideologies, structures, and practices in the U.S. have assumed a separation between theory and practice. From a human systems dynamics perspective, such a distinction is not possible. To build **coherence** in a complex system, the integration of theory and practice must be seamless—we learn by doing, and we teach by doing—in shared cycles of action and inquiry.	Praxis Loop Four Truths Architectural Model
Act with courage.	We certainly acknowledge that this approach to school transformation is radical. Typically, educators are not prone to risky decisions, but dealing with the uncertainty and inevitable change within complex adaptive systems requires **risk-taking**. Everyone in the system will benefit from being curious and courageous in the face of uncertainty.	Three Kinds of Change Adaptive Action for Uncertain Times
Engage in joyful practice.	Schools, regardless of their bureaucratic trappings, are places where human beings come together to teach and learn. If we don't find the experience **joyful, we will disengage, and the system will lose its vitality, its relevancy, and its capacity to adapt. Joyful practice is one key to sustaining engagement for everyone in the system.**	This simple rule can influence your use of any method or model.

In Chapter 1, we explain the power of simple rules in complex systems, and in each subsequent chapter, we discuss one simple rule, connecting it to one of these seven challenges for school reformers listed above. The Concluding Note emphasizes how these simple rules can contribute to our overarching goal--adaptive capacity throughout the system.

Each of these seven simple rules for generative teaching/learning and school transformation is important because they are interdependent and mutually reinforcing. If you want to shift the dynamics in a school system, you can begin with any of them—and the more rules you address, the greater chance for system-wide self-organization. And, of course, your conversations with students, colleagues, and parents about the rules and how to live them out in your school are at least as important as the rules themselves.

Our approach, grounded in human systems dynamics, is different from other approaches to school reforms (even those grounded in complexity and systems thinking) in three very important ways.

First, we offer explanations, rather than mere descriptions. Although many reformers offer vivid descriptions of promising and proven methods (lists of principles, guidelines, steps in the process), we offer explanations of how systems work--explanations of complex phenomena in non-technical language accessible to students, teachers, campus and district leaders, policy-makers, and the general public.

Second, we offer options for action, rather than lists of competencies or characteristics. The seven simple rules suggest actions that contribute to adaptive capacity. Teachers and administrators can use those general simple rules to generate specific rules that fit their jobs, their classrooms, their schools, and their communities.

Third, we show how individual adaptive capacity links to collective capacity throughout the system. Human systems dynamics asserts that the way to change systems is through local action by agents throughout the system—from bottom to top and from the inside out. When many people in the system begin acting according to shared understandings and agreements that focus on adaptation and responsiveness, new patterns will emerge, and the system's natural tendency to self-organize move it toward greater productivity and sustainability.

Each of you will come to this book with different objectives and expectations, and we urge you to think about your options in reading it.

- If you are engaged in a face-to-face or online HSD learning experience, you will use this book to supplement that experience. The chapters provide background and clarification for concepts encountered in your sessions.

- If you are interested in action steps, you might read Chapter 1 carefully and then consult the Table of Contents and the Appendix for methods and models that best address your particular challenges.

- If you are interested in what practitioners say about how these rules work for them, pay particular attention to the stories throughout the chapters. We have italicized those passages.

For further conversation with others throughout the HSD global network, see

- Human Systems Dynamics Institute http://www.hsdinstitute.org
- Human Systems Dynamics Institute Resources http://wiki.hsdinstitute.org/
- Adaptive Action Blog **http://AdaptiveAction.org**
- HSD Group on the *Literacy in Learning Exchange* http://www.literacyinlearningexchange.org/group/human-systems-dynamics-institute

Whatever your perspective and whatever your goals, we invite you into a lively inquiry about how we can work together to set conditions for widespread transformation of teaching and learning at all levels of schools.

Leslie Patterson
Royce Holladay
Glenda H. Eoyang

Contents

CHAPTER 1:
Simple (Yet Radical) Rules for Schools

This book is grounded in the field of human systems dynamics (HSD), a clear and simple way of seeing, understanding, and influencing the almost overwhelming challenges facing schools in the United States today. We offer seven simple rules to guide decisions about teaching and learning—rules that hold the potential for building adaptive capacity among educators, students, parents, and anyone interested in the radical transformation of schooling.

Central Challenge	Transforming schools by changing the way we think about teaching and learning
Concepts, Methods, and Models	<ul><li>Human Systems Dynamics</li><li>Complex adaptive system (CAS)</li><li>Adaptive capacity</li><li>Simple rules</li></ul>
Guiding Questions	<ul><li>What is human systems dynamics (HSD)?</li><li>What can HSD offer schools?</li><li>What is a complex adaptive system?</li><li>What is adaptive capacity?</li><li>What are simple rules?</li><li>So what simple rules now guide the status quo in schools?</li><li>Now what? Use simple rules to enhance adaptive capacity.</li><li>Now what? Use these resources to learn more.</li></ul>

Saul Alinsky, the long-time labor and civil rights organizer, published *Rules for Radicals: A Pragmatic Primer for Realistic Radicals* in 1971. In the book, he issues a call to action, reminding would-be reformers that, although their goals should be idealistic, their work must be grounded in a clear and unsentimental view of reality. In that spirit, we have written this book as a call to action for change agents in schools.

WHAT IS HUMAN SYSTEMS DYNAMICS (HSD)?

This book grew out of work led by Glenda Eoyang, one of the authors. In the early 1980s, as she was beginning to train and consult with corporate leaders, she saw challenges arising from complex economic realities, changing demographics, and shifting political ideologies. Her academic background in the philosophy of science allowed her to see and understand how researchers across multiple fields in both the physical and social sciences were beginning to study complex adaptive phenomena. Based on her investigation of complex systems in general and complex human systems in particular, she developed an approach that is now recognized as the field of "human systems dynamics" (HSD) (http://www.hsdinstitute.org/; Eoyang, 2002). On the HSD Institute website, Eoyang defines HSD as "a collection of concepts and tools that help make sense of the patterns that emerge from chaos when people work and play together in groups, families, organizations, and communities." Since founding the Institute in 2003, Glenda has trained over 350 HSD Associates in ten days of intensive instruction related to HSD theory and practice. She and this growing network of colleagues have developed a robust framework and a set of flexible methods/models—graphic representations of how HSD helps us "see, interpret, and influence" the patterns in our experiences.

Associates live and work in at least 15 countries around the world, including HSD centers in Minneapolis, Minnesota; London; and Tel Aviv. They use HSD methods and models across multiple disciplines: medicine, mathematics, computer programming, peace studies and conflict resolution, sustainable agriculture, electoral politics, public policy, organization development, program evaluation, human resources, and linguistics.

Royce and Leslie--the other two authors of this book—were early adopters of HSD. We are colleagues who are also sisters and, at family reunions over the years, we have enjoyed ongoing conversations about our work, about complex systems, and about Glenda's development of HSD. Each of us has used HSD in our work, sharing our insights and experiences, formulating shared questions, and challenging each other's

2

views. More recently we have found ways to bring our work together and have been collaborating in our applications of HSD in education settings.

In past lives, Royce has been a teacher, counselor, special education administrator, school district administrator, and strategic planner. In the mid-1990s, she and Glenda began applying complexity principles in her work as a district leader in large school districts. When Glenda founded the Human Systems Dynamics Institute, Royce began working more closely with her and the Institute. She now serves as the Director of the Network and Training at the Institute. She also consults with a range of organizations and develops materials and publications that contribute to HSD concepts and principles.

Leslie has worked as a literacy teacher, researcher, and teacher-educator, primarily in middle and high schools. For about 20 twenty years, her conversations with Glenda and Royce have richly informed this work. Recently, she has been more deliberate and explicit about using HSD methods and models in her research and practice related to literacy instruction, to action research, and to educational policy development. She also uses these principles to set conditions for learning in her university classes and in professional development communities.

Glenda has led our evolving understandings and practice while continuing her deep and wide inquiry into complex adaptive systems through her work as consultant. In 2011-12, we had the opportunity to collaborate with colleagues from The Ball Foundation (http://www.ballfoundation.org/ei/index.html) and the staff of New Haven Unified School District in California. Our shared goal was to help administrators and teachers across the system think more coherently about their work—with the ultimate goal of improving student learning. The theory and practice reflected in this work began in multiple places and experiences, but it emerged more fully and explicitly through this collaboration. Kari McVeigh, the superintendent, and Wendy Gudalewicz, the Chief Academic Officer, had come to the district two years prior to this project, and they were introducing structures, processes, and instructional approaches that would support a system-wide focus on student learning, with a priority on literacy teaching and learning. We are deeply thankful for the opportunity to learn alongside them.

What Can HSD Offer Schools?

After almost three decades of unrelenting headlines about the disastrous condition of public schools in the U.S., we might wonder how these schools are still in business. How could any institution in so much trouble actually survive? Perhaps, as some argue, this is a "manufactured crisis" (Berliner & Biddle, 1995)—a politically inspired blame game designed to put particular individuals in office and to create a profit for others. This blame game goes something like this: We blame schools (and teachers) for students' poor achievement, and we look for a politician, policy, or profit-making scheme that will save the day. When that reform falls short of its promise, we blame schools (and teachers) for failing to implement it successfully. We then look to yet another politician (or policy or profit-making scheme) as the next salvation. And so on.

That blame game is clearly in play, but it is not the whole story. The current state of public schools is, in fact, disappointing. Student engagement, attention to students' home cultures, response to diverse learning needs, the efficient use of resources, and teacher professionalism are just a few of the areas where reformers continue to be frustrated. Although astounding success stories and "pockets of excellence" have come from reform initiatives, no one is arguing that reform movements have been an unqualified success. In fact, there is an emerging critique of the recent standards movement and the high stakes testing regimens, both of which are ubiquitous in the current system and seem to have yielded disappointing results.

Some of the problems and challenges facing educators can be traced to poor administrative or instructional decisions, but some emerge from larger societal issues and have been exacerbated by policies and regulations that mandate particular solutions. For example, unsustainable market forces (the profit motive, consumerism, competition, neoliberalism, labor/management conflicts) permeate public discourse and policy at all levels. In addition, globalization has had far-reaching economic, cultural, and political implications. Rapidly changing information technologies introduce additional pressures and possibilities. Shifting employment patterns and the recent financial crisis mean that too many children live in poverty in the U.S. Finally, the so-called cultural wars emerging from our increasing ethnic, linguistic, and cultural diversities and our polarizing, ideological discourse contribute to the challenges. All these economic, environmental, political, cultural, and ethical challenges resist simplistic solutions.

The recent wave of school reform, beginning with the Reagan-era publication of *Nation at Risk*, has attempted to address these issues. Reform initiatives have included state and national standards, tests, high stakes accountability schemes, standardized curricula, and incentives for teacher quality. Although the public discourse focused on a commitment to high standards for all students, it is clear that political ambition and the profit motive have also been significant drivers of these reform efforts. The influence on public schools has been dramatic. Not only has this standards-based movement somehow trumped the long-standing tradition of local school control in the U.S., it has also been accompanied by a dramatic surge in privatization, home-schooling, and charter schools. In addition, the recent global financial crisis has decimated state and local school budgets. It is not an overstatement to say that many U.S. schools are, in fact, in crisis.

Through media campaigns like the one surrounding the 2010 documentary *Waiting for Superman* (Chilton, 2010), the public has been led to think that the problem with the nation's schools is educators in general and teachers in particular. President Obama's "Blueprint" for the reauthorization of the Elementary and Secondary Education Act replaced former President Bush's "No Child Left Behind." Though emphasizing slightly different initiatives, both were based on the implementation of standards, high stakes accountability, and the evaluation of schools and teachers using standardized tests scores. Although high-profile critics of this approach, like Diane Ravitch (2011), are beginning to exert some influence, this absolute faith in external mandates is still pervasive. The problems and challenges persist. This list of policy moves based on this approach gives a sense of the status quo:

- Standards for student performance
- High stakes tests
- Incentives for innovations to raise test scores
- "Evidence-based" programs that standardize instructional decisions
- Accountability schemes that make test scores public
- Public funds for charter schools
- Alternative routes for teacher certification
- Teacher evaluation based on test scores.

Not only are these policies not solving the problems, they seem to trigger unpredicted consequences as problematic as the issues that initially prompted the reforms!

We argue that these reform initiatives, no matter how well intended or faithfully implemented, simply offer the wrong tools for the task. They respond to descriptions of what is "wrong," but cannot address underlying reasons or dynamics that prevent or limit learning. They identify a broad list of issues that are not working and attempt to "fix" them with short-sighted and sometimes complicated interventions. We believe that these approaches to reform emerge from ineffective and inappropriate beliefs and understandings about complex systems. We agree with the growing numbers of reformers who recommend systems approaches. "Much that happens in schools can be understood only by understanding how the social systems that comprise schools operate. This is why systems thinking is so important to educational leaders" (Schlechty, 2009, p. 25).

The most recent reform initiatives grounded in high stakes accountability are not grounded in systems thinking and, in fact, they recommend the wrong rules for guiding our collective learning and decision-making. In this book we offer an alternative way to think and work in schools—and an alternative set of "simple rules" that can support student learning and help schools thrive.

Human systems dynamics is grounded in the study of self-organizing systems. Researchers have observed that agents within these complex systems operate according to a short set of simple rules—rules which emerge from the system and which subsequently influence the system's future path (Reynolds, 1987). The content of the rules may vary, depending on the goals and constraints in the system. An HSD approach to system transformation acknowledges that these simple rules influence the system. HSD suggests models and methods that can either reinforce old rules that seem to be productive or generate new rules that are more in line with shared goals. In other words, HSD methods and models are designed to strengthen the rules that hold the potential for establishing more generative and sustainable patterns in the system. (Figure 1.1)

These generative patterns can lead to "whole system reform," as Fullan calls this kind of self-organizing change. As he says in *All System Go* (2010), "When it works, and I am talking practically, amazing things get accomplished with less effort; or more accurately, wasted effort gives way to energizing action" (p.3).

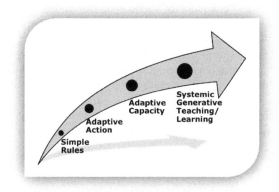

Figure 1.1: Simple rules as starting point for Systemic Generative Teaching/Learning. Simple rules inform decision making in Adaptive Action, which builds Adaptive Capacity. When an education system builds Adaptive Capacity at all scales, it engages in Systemic Generative Teaching/Learning.

In this book, we recommend seven particular simple rules and argue that these rules have led to sustainable learning systems in the K-12 schools where we have worked. These rules respond to the need for setting conditions for collective capacity (Fullan, 2010) and sustainability (Hargreaves and Fink, 2006) in schools. They are grounded both in our understanding of complex adaptive systems and in our experiences watching educators use these as guidelines for teaching and learning.

We call these rules "radical" for two reasons. First, radical refers to that which is fundamental or essential--addressing the root, or the source. These are radical rules because they address the underlying, root dynamics of a sustainable, generative teaching/learning system. Second, these rules are radical because they call for a revolutionary mindset and for extreme methods, vastly different from the status quo.

Before we discuss those particular rules, it is important to understand more about how complex adaptive systems, or self-organizing systems, work.

WHAT IS A COMPLEX ADAPTIVE SYSTEM?

We sometimes hear teachers say that a class of students has "taken on a life of its own." This happens because students, classes, and schools (like families, organizations, communities, and cultures) are complex, adaptive, and self-organizing systems. Dooley defines "complex adaptive system" as a "collection of agents (people, groups, ideas) that interact so that system-wide patterns emerge, and those patterns subsequently act on and influence the interactions among the agents" (Dooley, 1996) (see Figure 1.2). That certainly fits the school systems we know. Students in a classroom interact in such a way that a classroom culture (system-wide patterns) develops. Over time, the norms and expectations (patterns) of that culture begin to influence the behaviors of the students in the class, by reinforcing those behaviors that match the culture or by punishing or ignoring the behaviors that don't match the culture.

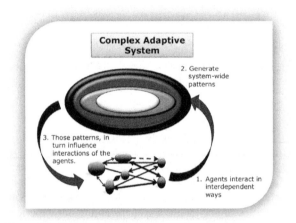

Figure 1.2: Emergent patterns in a complex adaptive system (CAS). Agents interact, which creates system-wide patterns that subsequently influence the agents' interactions.

Here is a how a middle school science teacher describes the complex adaptive systems in which she works:

> *I see several complex adaptive systems in my work: my classroom, the science department, the eighth grade team, the District Education Improvement Committee of which I am a member, and even my cheerleading squad. Each class period has its own personality, and, as a result, I adapt each period and each day. There are different stakeholders to whom the students and I report, including the principal, the assistant principals, the counselors, the parents, and even other teachers. The science department is a complex adaptive system because there are multiple layers of organization: the department head, the district*

*science coordinator, the grade level leader, the principal
and vice principal, the state education agency, the
curriculum director, and the superintendent. We are
constantly having to adapt to changes. If a lesson or
lab isn't working, we have to learn and adapt and attempt
to go about it another way. Often we do not have adequate
funding for lab supplies, and we will have to improvise as
we go along and share information and ideas that work or
do not work. Our science coordinator sometimes does not
provide correct district assessments or deliver needed
items on time. Again, we are forced to improvise and adapt
as a team.*

—Middle School Science Teacher

As a complex adaptive system (CAS), a school has more in common with an ecosystem than with the most complicated machine you can imagine. Zoom in on a single student, and you can focus on the complexity within any human being. In fact, learning is itself a complex adaptive process (many different experiences in motion, interacting and coming together in patterns of meaning). Zoom out to consider the whole district, and you can see the same amazing complexity (many interdependent parts/agents always in motion). Schools and the larger community are comprised of many interdependent, overlapping, and nested systems, all of which continually adapt to changes within their boundaries and in the environment that holds them.

Time Out for Reflection
*Think about the complex adaptive systems where you live and work.
Focus on one of them. Who are the agents? How do they interact?
What patterns emerge in those interactions? How do those patterns
influence subsequent interactions?*

We are not alone in pointing out these interdependent relationships among various systems and subsystems that influence schools (see, for example, Crowell and Reid-Marr, 2013; Davis and Sumara, 2006 and Doll and colleagues, 2008). Schlechty says, "The link between the quality of schools and the quality of community life is so deep and profound that it makes no sense to work to improve the schools outside the context of improving communities as well" (2009, p. xi). When we see all these as complex adaptive systems, we assume that, as students, parents, teachers, administrators, librarians, counselors, custodians, bus drivers, school board members, merchants, community volunteers, and policy makers interact, patterns of attitudes, behavior, and communication emerge. Sometimes those patterns emerge in ways that support powerful learning for all students; sometimes they don't.

The focus of this book is to help us all watch for these patterns, make sense of them, and then work together to reinforce (or generate) the patterns that support learning.

WHAT IS ADAPTIVE CAPACITY?

When we thoughtfully and deliberately watch for patterns in the behaviors of our students and colleagues, interpret those patterns, and take action to reinforce what we see as supportive and productive patterns, we are taking Adaptive Action. Adaptive Action is an inquiry/action process that is natural and essential to human life. Here is a simple way to think about this process. We pay attention to our experiences and to the world around us, and we say,

- **WHAT** is happening?
- **SO WHAT** does it mean?
- **NOW WHAT** shall I/we do about it?

This deceptively simple inquiry cycle is a springboard to action and to questions that can lead us directly into another cycle. These three questions—framed as **Adaptive Action**—are central to learning, to change in human systems (Eoyang and Holladay, 2013). The rest of this book, especially Chapter 2, explores Adaptive Action in much more detail.

We believe that Adaptive Action is essential to building and sustaining productive, resilient, and generative systems. We also believe that, over time, individuals and groups can build dispositions, skills, and organizational structures to facilitate Adaptive Action across and up and down the larger system. When Adaptive Action becomes a way of life throughout a system, we can say that this system has **adaptive capacity**.

In schools, adaptive capacity (in individual learners, in classrooms, among faculty and staff, in family connections, and in community stakeholder groups) leads to rich and productive learning experiences for everyone involved. We call that kind of experience **generative teaching/learning**. Chapter 2 focuses more on what we mean by that term, but for our purposes at this point, we can say that generative teaching/learning is a way to talk about transformational experiences that 1) fulfill the emotional, cognitive, and physical needs of individuals, and 2) set conditions for ongoing adaptation, action, and inquiry that will sustain the system over time. The products of generative teaching/learning will appear in the system in ways that can be assessed and measured. The most

10

important, of course, would be improvements in student engagement and, ultimately, student achievement.

This book argues for seven simple rules that have proven useful to educators who want to engage in Adaptive Action, build adaptive capacity throughout the system, and sustain generative teaching/learning to improve student achievement (see Figure 1.1).

WHAT ARE SIMPLE RULES?

System-wide **patterns** that are so strong they influence our actions (for better or worse), are shaped by the agents' agreement—sometimes overt, but often tacit—to live according to a shared set of "simple rules." To understand and use simple rules, we need to understand more about how **patterns** emerge in our complex adaptive systems.

Think of the patterns in a beautiful Persian rug. We notice similarities—shapes and colors that are repeated across the rug. But we also notice differences. The contrasts in the colors and shapes make the design recognizable and (usually) pleasing to the eye. What makes the design beautiful (or not) is how the artist connects these similarities and differences in unique ways. The beauty of the rug and our individual perceptions of the rug emerge from the connections (interactions) among these similarities and differences in the colors, shapes, and textures. We are surrounded by patterns like these—similarities, differences, and connections—and the patterns in human life are in motion, not still. We perceive them as videos, not snapshots. We perceive these patterns as art, music, wisdom, friendship, ambition, joy—just to name a few of the patterns in human experience. All of these patterns emerge from **similarities, differences, and connections that have meaning across space and time**. That is how we define "pattern" in HSD (Eoyang and Holladay, 2013).

Now, let's think about patterns in schools. We can notice similarities in the ways people in schools act, but there are also differences grounded in their unique histories, their challenges, their capacities, and their identities. There are connections within, between, and among them. Patterns are generated by these similarities, differences and connections. We might refer to the dominant patterns on a campus as the "campus culture." When we talk about "building community," we are talking about encouraging certain patterns and discouraging others. We might look for patterns of "student engagement" or patterns of "trust" that encourage patterns of "risk-taking." One way to think about school transformation is to think about how we can strengthen the patterns that support generative teaching and learning and how to extinguish non-generative patterns.

(Throughout the book, we refer to **"generative" teaching/learning** as responsive, adaptive, and creative. Chapter 2 addresses it in more detail.)

Patterns bring **coherence** to the system. As patterns form, some become more pronounced. **Simple rules** emerge from a system as people begin building shared perspectives and shared repertoires of practices. As the simple rules emerge, they influence the changes across the whole system, as well as i how individual agents function. Subsequently, other patterns may emerge as these simple rules further influence the dynamics of the system.

> *I work in the central office of an urban district. One of our positive patterns is collaboration. This is definitely a positive pattern of behavior that supports conversations with colleagues across divisions in an effort to provide support for all students. We also collaborate with parents-- especially parents whose first language is not English. . .our district makes a tremendous effort to collaborate with parents. As a result, our parents are very willing to participate in meetings, volunteer and attend special functions for their children.*

> *Within my own team, however, there is a deep pattern based on peer relationships. Several of my colleagues have worked together for many years and socialize outside the job. I've noticed that their friendship sometimes takes priority over student outcomes. The ideas and opinions of those of us outside this friendship circle are often dismissed. I find this disheartening. This pattern of considering adult relationships over students' needs does cause considerable mistrust and interferes with the larger pattern of collaboration that I see in our work with colleagues with parents.*

> *—District Office Instructional Coordinator*

In other words, patterns of behavior are generated when people follow a short list of simple rules. The simple rules tend to set conditions for self-organization, and they also reinforce those conditions as time goes on (Holladay, 2002). Whether the rules are implicit and unspoken or explicit and widely known, they help individuals function together to live out the foundational beliefs and values of the organization. Simple rules are like the DNA in living organisms, carrying the code that governs how organs and cells are built and how they work in the human body. As the code is generated and copied, it leads to differentiation and development. In much the same way, simple rules can be thought of as carrying the codes that make up relationships and work expectations as they are iterated through organizational and individual decisions.

It certainly makes common sense to talk about rules emerging from human systems. For example, conventional ways to use grammar in a particular language emerge over many years as people use that language. We can see that happening now as people develop particular ways of formulating text messages. We can also see that cultural "norms" are simple rules that emerge from the ways people relate to one another in particular settings over time. Customs and rituals also involve "simple rules" about how to behave alone and together. All of these patterns come from the dynamics within the system; they are not instituted by committee actions, nor are they imposed from the outside.

When simple rules are explicit and generative, everyone in a classroom, across a campus, or throughout a school district agrees to follow a common set of simple rules they have decided will encourage and sustain learning. When that is the case, everyone benefits. An explicit set of generative simple rules can support schools in several ways:

- Teachers, students, administrators, and staff are better able to anticipate what others will do, so they experience more trust, cohesiveness, and consistency.

- Because of this cohesiveness, there is less need to codify all decisions and contingencies, so there is less need for layers of bureaucracy.

- Organizational structures and procedures will ultimately be aligned with the simple rules, so everyone can focus on student learning more efficiently and effectively.

- Because simple rules continue across time, they assure continuity through the hard times, for example, when a charismatic leader moves on or when resources are scarce.

- As individuals interact according to simple rules, patterns of behavior emerge, forming the culture of the organization. By searching for the simple rules at work, leaders can understand the foundational elements of the system's culture. By leading the group to build a list of simple rules to guide their work, leaders can communicate organizational values in ways that are actionable.

- Simple rules establish organizational expectations for performance and behavior and are "portable," meaning they can be shared throughout the organization.

Some people express concern that this is "just one more list of rules" in organizations that are already overrun with regulations and procedures. If the word "rule" has distracting connotations for a group, they can certainly be called something else. Some suggestions for alternative names for simple rules might include "norms," "expectations," "beliefs," or "values."

The difficulty with those words is that, just as with "rules," each has its own connotations. Norms may seem to be too informal, like short-term expectations created for a meeting. "Expectations" may work, but they are often more specific to one situation than the simple rules, which should generalize to any situation. "Beliefs" or "values" are different in kind. They name concepts—"Here is what I believe or value,"—while simple rules indicate behavior—"Here is what I do to live according to a particular belief." Simple rules begin with action verbs to say that they are about doing, rather than believing. Names carry weight, and it is important that simple rules retain their power to inform and influence behavior, regardless of what they are called. One group we worked with decided to call them "seed behaviors" because they felt they were planting the seeds from which their new culture could grow.

To begin a conversation about developing simple rules, questions are key. "How do we want to operate with each other around here?" "What is really important to us as a team?" "How do we want to treat our coworkers and our community or customers?" These questions will lead to those few critical behaviors that can become the simple rules. Here are a few "rules" to remember about developing simple rules (Eoyang, 1997).

- The rules should be designed to amplify and reward desired behaviors.

- The rules should be kept to "Minimum Specifications." The statements should be brief and powerful.

- They should also be transferable across the organization. If a rule applies only in one or two places in the organization, then it is an instruction, not a rule. To identify the rule underneath that instruction, people should ask why that is important. What is the ultimate goal of such an instruction? The rule that underlies that instruction will become explicit.

- The list should be short. There should be five (plus or minus two) rules as a maximum, and the fewer that can be named and still capture the intent of the organization, the better. A short list is important for a couple of reasons. It is generally accepted that humans cannot remember more than about seven items in a list, and if simple rules are to guide individual behaviors, they should be easy to remember. Additionally, reducing the list to such a small number forces groups to clarify the real simple rules.

- Simple rules should address three important areas of relationship within the organization. First, at least one rule should address why people come together and who they are as a group—the container that bounds them. Second, there should be at least one rule to address the significant differences in the work. Then at least one rule should focus on how people exchange information and other resources. (We will discuss these three areas in more detail in Chapter 4.)

- Each rule should begin with an action verb. Most value statements are passive descriptions of what is important, leaving a gap between them and the action of the organization. If there are action-oriented statements about how to live those values, however, the expectations are more clear.

Finally, simply stating the list of simple rules (and posting them on a website or on the classroom wall) is not enough to create the desired patterns of interaction across the organization. It is critical that the rules be discussed and implemented in myriad ways over time, by every person in the system. Here are some ways to do this:

- Invite people to talk about what a particular simple rule means to them in their own job responsibilities.

- Develop explicit descriptions of what people expect to see and experience as a result of using each simple rule in different aspects of their work.

- Use one or more simple rule to evaluate outcomes of meetings or other events.

- Post the simple rules at the bottom of the agendas of meetings to ensure easy access and recall for decision making throughout the dialogue.

So What Simple Rules Now Guide the Status Quo in Schools?

We would argue that certain simple rules have emerged over the years and have generated patterns that have very strong influence over what happens in schools. We further argue that the influence of these simple rules is so strong that it is difficult NOT to go along with them. We tend to perpetuate particular practices, even when it becomes clear that these behaviors are no longer functional for the system or supportive of student learning.

For example, in the middle of the twentieth century, schools began the practice of using test results to assign students to particular programs or instructional treatments. The unspoken simple rule that shaped that pattern probably went something like this, "Serve students according to need." Federal mandates and funding schemes reinforced this rule; teacher educators generated certifications for these new programs; and publishers rushed to provide materials for this emerging market. The field of "Special Education" emerged. For years, educators administered tests and placed students according to that simple rule, never questioning its implications. Although we saw many beneficial results, eventually, we realized that this simple rule also led to unintended consequences that were potentially hurtful and or damaging to students. Perhaps because of the deficit perspective inherent in focusing primarily on "need," students were sometimes inappropriately labeled, teachers were overwhelmed with paperwork; students' strengths were not taken into account. Some who questioned the use of that rule were quashed by the system, and their voices were marginalized. We continue to struggle with modifying or adjusting that simple rule so that all students—regardless of their strengths and needs—can engage in powerful learning experiences.

As we pointed out above, the conversations about the simple rules (existing or desired) are as important as the rules themselves. This story about a group of teachers and administrators illustrates how their conversations helped them recognize some dysfunctional simple rules at work in their system:

> *In working with staff in a mid-sized district where people were experiencing some frustration in their restructuring process, we introduced simple rules as a tool for analyzing how school staff members were working toward their goals. For several meetings, across several days, the conversations seemed to be "stuck." People told stories about their frustrations, they referred to the official list of district priorities, and they tried to*

*identify the underlying issues. But we continued to struggle. At
some point, one of them asked, "What ARE our simple rules?"*

*Everyone was silent. Finally, another person spoke up, "We'll
have to be honest."*

*Another silence. A different person spoke, "Let's just do it.
Let's just level with each other about what our students need
and what we are willing to do about it."*

*At that point the tension broke; everyone leaned forward,
began talking, and within 10 minutes they had generated a list
of simple rules that fit their experiences and that suggested
some options for action.*

*Two of the long-standing and somewhat dysfunctional simple
rules this group identified were, "Take care of your own," and
"Make nice." The first rule meant that many actions across the
district could be attributed to people focusing on their
individual campus needs. This clearly worked against district-
wide coherence and trust, regardless of how often and how
loudly the administrators talked about a unified, collaborative
approach. The second rule meant that no one felt comfortable
with public disagreement or confrontation. This rule
discouraged difficult conversations about significant issues that
colleagues really needed to sort out.*

*This conversation about the simple rules was a breakthrough.
It made it possible for these colleagues to think about the
patterns they wanted to see in their work across the district and
about what alternative simple rules might set the conditions for
patterns they wanted to see.*

Schools contain multiple massively entangled human systems—
individuals, peer groups, grade levels, classes, faculties, committees,
neighbors, extracurricular teams, parent organizations—all of which have
histories and agendas for the future. In these systems, we see evidence of
deep-rooted expectations, norms, rituals, roles, biases, goals,
understandings, perceptions—all of which enforce particular ways of
behaving over time, which we are calling simple rules. Earlier, we said that
school reform initiatives, no matter how well intended, have simply not
been sufficient. Perhaps we should examine the simple rules that generate
persistent patterns to think about how they might be interfering with
teaching and learning.

Here are some simple rules that we have seen at work in the status
quo—simple rules that are seldom spoken and may be operating below a

conscious level. We believe these rules cannot support adaptive learning and, therefore, are not sustainable in complex adaptive systems.

- Change the system gradually--one piece at a time.
- Fix the people first.
- Consult the experts.
- Implement with fidelity.
- Don't ask questions.
- Don't challenge authority.
- Don't rock the boat.
- Focus on what works, not why it works.
- Find and fix root causes.

These rules do not broaden and deepen systemic adaptation to cultural and social realities. They do not help us understand the systems where we live and work. They do not help us identify what is important and take steps toward that. They do not help us set the conditions for productive and emergent patterns of interaction and performance. What they do is stifle individual and group creativity, expression, and the potential for adaptation. They ignore the interconnectedness and interdependence that characterize human systems. They focus on blaming rather than on finding solutions. They are not generative.

The real crisis in schools is not reflected in sound bites on cable news channels. It is not just about test scores or achievement gaps or student safety. It is not just about holding teachers, principals, and students accountable for working harder or smarter to produce higher test scores. Both the problems and the solutions are more complex than that. The real crisis in schools is that policy-makers tend to operate according to simple rules that impose short-sighted strategies for control and for short-term gains—whether annual gains in test scores or political advantage in the next election cycle. Current simple rules in schools shape strategies that tend not to catalyze the strengths and energy inherent in the system. They do not invite or support the kind of transformative learning that both builds on and sustains the complex, self-organizing dynamics of learning or the environments that encourage learning.

Time Out for Reflection
Think about one of your most persistent challenges. What dysfunctional simple rules might be at work in your system? Are any of the dysfunctional rules listed above relevant? What patterns result, and what might you do to make a difference?

NOW WHAT? USE SIMPLE RULES TO ENHANCE ADAPTIVE CAPACITY

We don't pretend to know what structures, programs, approaches, routines, procedures, or regulations will best support teaching and learning in schools five or ten or fifty years from now. The best we can do is agree on a set of simple rules that make it possible for the system (and the people in the system) to adapt and transform as the challenges continue to evolve. We agree with Schlechty (2009):

> If the performance of America's schools is to improve, it is essential that the schools have the capacity to innovate on a continuous basis and in a disciplined way. Bureaucracies lack this capacity. Continuous innovation is the lifeblood of learning organizations. . . (pp. 223-224).

In Chapters 2-8, we suggest seven simple rules that hold the potential for continuous adaptation and transformation—for adaptive capacity. Each chapter focuses on one of these simple rules, each providing an explanation, illustrations, methods, models, and resources for further inquiry. We recommend these seven simple rules:

- Teach and learn in every interaction.
- See, understand, and influence patterns.
- Pay attention to patterns in the whole, the part, and the greater whole.
- Recognize and build on assets of self and others.
- Search for the true and the useful.
- Act with courage.
- Engage in joyful practice.

Each rule contributes to the dynamics of a sustainable teaching/learning system in unique and important ways. These rules are interdependent, and no one rule is more important than any other. Together, they suggest options for action--ways we can work together to transform teaching and learning in schools.

NOW WHAT? USE THESE RESOURCES TO LEARN MORE

Alinsky, S. (1972). Rules for radicals: A pragmatic primer for realistic radicals. New York: Random House.

Conway, J. Game of Life. http://www.bitstorm.org/gameoflife/ and http://www.math.com/students/wonders/life/life.html

Holladay, R. (2005). Simple rules: Organizational DNA. *ODPractitioner, 37,* 4, 29-34

Holland, J. (1999). *Emergence: From chaos to order.* NY: Basic Books.

Josić, K. (2012). Complexity and emergence. No. 2553. From *Engines of our Ingenuity.* http://www.uh.edu/engines/epi2553.htm

Nova. (2007). *Emergence: Q&A with John Holland.* http://www.pbs.org/wgbh/nova/nature/holland-emergence.html

Resnick, M. and Silverman, B. Exploring emergence. http://www.playfulinvention.com/emergence/contents.html

Serendip. http://serendip.brynmawr.edu/complexity/

Simple Rules Foundation. http://simplerulesfoundation.org/

Tytel, M. & Holladay, R. (2011). *Simple rules: A radical inquiry into self: Going beyond self-help, discover your ability to change the world and generate self-hope.* Apache Junction, AZ: Gold Canyon Press.

Tytel, M. & Holladay, R. (2011). *Radical inquiry journal: A companion tool for simple rules, a radical inquiry into self.* Apache Junction, AZ: Gold Canyon Press.

CHAPTER 2:
Generative Teaching/Learning

Simple Rule:
Teach and learn in every interaction.

Teaching and learning are our central business and our passion. In complex systems, teaching and learning make adaptation possible. Complex adaptive teaching/learning build on what the system already "knows," as well as generating new questions, new understandings, and new options for action. This chapter explains how generative teaching/learning can set conditions for school transformation and suggests that Adaptive Action makes generative teaching and learning a way of life in schools.

Central Challenge	Invite and support learner engagement.
Simple Rule	Teach and learn in every interaction.
Concepts, Methods, and Models	• Generative Teaching/Learning • Adaptive Action • Learner's Landscape
Guiding Questions	• What is generative teaching/learning? • What is Adaptive Action? • What are teachers' and learners' roles? • So what about student engagement? • Now what? Teach and learn to enhance adaptive capacity. • Now what? Use these resources to learn more.

Our work in schools has taught us something about what happens when people take an inquiry stance toward their work—when they commit to teaching and learning together. This quote from a literacy coach in an elementary school hints at this power:

> *When you work as an instructional coach, the perception is often that you're coming in as an expert, even though you say you're not. We're learning together, we're growing together. But the teachers still want answers. So asking the questions and looking at patterns together has been my focus now as I work with teachers. And it has kind of naturally just developed. In the beginning of the year, they were saying things like "Oh, come on. Just give me the answers." And now it's more, "OK. I know this is what we do now. We do a cycle of inquiry." We ask questions and work together, and it's not this top-down type of thing. It's not "I'm an expert; you're going to learn from me . . ."*

> *—Literacy Coach*

In Chapter 1, we talked about schools as networks of complex, nonlinear, and adaptive systems. In this chapter, we explore teaching and learning as complex, adaptive processes. Although we see ALL learning as complex and adaptive, we know that it can look quite different in a kindergarten block center, in a fifth-grade language arts class, on a soccer field, in an SAT preparation session, and in a professional development session for teachers. We want to focus on the kind of teaching and learning that we want to see in all these contexts—when learners are genuinely engaged, making connections with background knowledge and finding new patterns in their experiences—patterns that bring increasing coherence across the whole system. We would say that this kind of teaching and learning is **generative**, and we argue that generative teaching/learning is connected to **adaptive capacity**. Adaptive capacity promotes system vitality and sustainability (generativity). The simple rule that promotes generative teaching/learning is this:

Teach and learn in every interaction.

This kind of learning has long been the goal of progressive educators from Dewey forward. The digital revolution, of course, has exploded into possibilities for teaching and learning that we are just now imagining. The Internet has opened possibilities for this kind of learning across time and space, where learners of all ages can meet up to ask questions and solve problems of all kinds. It is difficult to represent this kind of vibrant, interactive learning on the two-dimensional pages of this book, but here are some websites that suggest the possibilities:

- connectedlearning.tv
- http://dmlcentral.net/
- http://digitalis.nwp.org/
- http://thebelab.blogspot.com/

(All retrieved January 25, 2013)

Competing learning theories have historically taken a position along a continuum between two extremes—one that views learners as passive recipients of knowledge and another that views learners as creative inquirers who create knowledge together. The tension among those competing perspectives plays out in a number of dichotomies that are familiar to most educators:

- Constructivism versus behaviorism
- Student-centered versus teacher-directed instruction
- Informal acquisition versus deliberate and explicit learning
- Focus on process versus product
- Inquiry versus explicit instruction
- Performance on authentic tasks versus test results

Because we are convinced that teaching and learning are complex processes that adapt to various constraints from within and outside the system, we reject these dualities and the either/or thinking that goes along with them. In fact, throughout this book, we assume that both extremes of each of these continua can be useful, depending on the context or purpose or participants. Each builds on and contains the other. We see them working in dialectical relationship. In other words, although they are apparently opposing perspectives, both are "true" and "appropriate," depending on particular conditions and contexts, and each perspective informs the other. And the tension between the extremes generates energy in the system. In human systems dynamics, we refer to these as **interdependent pairs** and use them to help us understand the systems where we work, teach, and learn.

We try to capture these apparent oppositions by focusing at once on both teaching and on learning. We view teaching and learning as integrated and mutually supporting, two perspectives on the same phenomenon. That's why we began with the quote from the instructional coach above. She is pointing to generative teaching/learning in her work.

WHAT IS GENERATIVE TEACHING/LEARNING?

What does it mean to teach and learn in a complex human system (CAS)? Remember from Chapter 1 that our definition of CAS is a "collection of agents (people, groups, ideas) that interact so that system-wide patterns emerge, and those patterns subsequently act on and influence the behaviors of the agents." When we apply that definition to learning, we might say that learning is the process through which ideas (experiences, knowledge, and perceptions, etc.) interact so that system-wide patterns emerge, and those patterns (concepts, principles, hypotheses, new questions, *etc.)* influence subsequent thought and action.

Figure 2.1 represents that ever-emergent and nonlinear process.

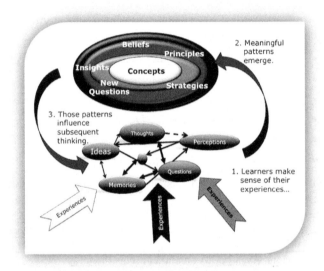

Figure 2.1: Learning as a complex adaptive process. Learners' thoughts interact to make meaningful patterns, and those patterns subsequently influence future thought and action.

Complex adaptive learning systems (brains and/or minds, individuals, and organizations) are open systems, open to new information and energy from the environment, and various ideas and facts interact as agents in the system (Davis and Sumara, 2006). They are also diverse, and they are nonlinear. Patterns help us make sense of this complexity. As scientists have pointed out, the essential function of the human brain is pattern-recognition (e.g., Coen, 2012; Johnson, 2001; Rose, 1997). When patterns are not clear, when we are challenged by new information, or when we face an anomaly, tension builds in the system. To relieve or resolve that tension, we search for coherent patterns. (That may be a conscious and deliberate search, or our brains may do it at a subconscious level, without our conscious control.) As we think (search for patterns), our ideas, feelings, questions, insights, and puzzles interact in unpredictable ways until system-wide patterns emerge in response to new information, perspectives, and experiences. These new patterns or insights shape further experience and the patterns that subsequently emerge.

This ongoing, recursive process through which new patterns emerge is "learning." The new patterns are what we have "learned." We believe that all learning is generative, and we use "generative" as a modifier to make a distinction between this complex adaptive perspective and other definitions of learning grounded in alternative paradigms.

Generative teaching/learning is not a method, approach, or program; it names a paradigm, a perspective—a particular way of approaching human learning. It assumes that we are all teachers AND learners in networks of complex adaptive systems. It assumes that teaching and learning are central to the way human beings navigate this complexity. It assumes that teaching and learning generate appropriate possibilities for moving forward into the unfamiliar and confusing future—new insights and new options for action. It assumes that we approach the world in particular ways:

- Curiosity rather than judgment.
- Questions rather than answers.
- Mutual exploration rather than conflict.
- Self-reflection rather than defensiveness.
- Attention to the dynamics of a challenge rather than its outcomes, process, or symptoms.
- Openness that emphasizes assets rather than rigid expectations and stereotypes.
- Recognition of potential for learning and growth that lies in every moment and interaction, rather than an intent to fix what's broken.

Time Out for Reflection
Think about your most powerful learning experiences, either inside or outside a classroom. Consider the description of generative learning. How does it compare to your experiences with teaching and learning? What can happen when people approach new experiences with this stance? What can happen if teachers and learners take a less generative stance?

Human systems dynamics practitioners often talk about "standing in inquiry" as they face novel or perplexing challenges. Some say that is the most powerful shift that HSD has helped them make in their work.

> *I think I can speak for myself and people on my campus when I say that the patterns around classroom discipline have shifted because we're now standing in inquiry. Maybe there's a kid who's off task in my class, and I don't say, "What's wrong with you?" It's not "You're wrong, get out of here". It's more like "Hey, can we chat outside for a minute? Tell me what's going on. What's happening right now? Is everything OK? Do you need five minutes? Do you need support? I have shifted, and I know others at my site have. HSD came at the perfect time because, because of budget cuts, we lost a teacher, we lost an AP, and we almost lost a counselor, so we all had to fill in those gaps. And this is a much more constructive way to deal with management and discipline.*

> *—Secondary Teacher*

This general perspective on teaching and learning is not unique to HSD. It is consistent with a number of perspectives from multiple disciplines—perspectives that carry labels like "progressive," "student-centered," "inquiry-based," "child-centered," "authentic," "culturally responsive," "whole language," and "problem-based." All of those approaches are coherent with generative learning. We use the term "generative" because we want to avoid the debates about particular methodologies, routines, or materials. We want to focus, instead, on the underlying system dynamics common to all these approaches—approaches that acknowledge the openness, the diversity, the nonlinearity, and the unpredictability inherent in human learning.

The term "generative" to describe a perspective on learning is not original with us. For example, Wittrock referred to "Generative Learning Theory" as "processes that people use actively and dynamically to (a) select events and (b) generate meaning for events" (1992, p. 532). The assumption is that learning is an active process; learners are meaning-making agents. People use their background knowledge, experiences, attitudes and perceptions to see and understand patterns in their experiences. Those emerging understandings lead to subsequent action and experience from which learners make additional meanings.

In 1950, the psychoanalyst Erikson hinted at this adaptation toward coherence when he used the term "generativity" to talk about a mature individual's concern for guiding the next generation. For Erickson, "generativity" described the stage of development when adults try to "make a difference", to "give back," to "take care" of their communities. That use of the term clearly supports our focus on both responsiveness and adaptation toward coherence (Erickson, 1950, 242.

In 2008, Zittrain used the term "generativity" to refer to Internet-based products that provide platforms on which users can build new applications or run new protocols without permission, referring to a system's capacity to produce unanticipated change through contributions from broad and varied audiences. As we apply this concept to learning, we would agree with Zittrain that we would expect to see openness, unpredictability, and the emergence of unanticipated structures, or creativity.

In the 1990s we again see "generative" applied to the themes that invite students into problem-posing inquiry (Shor, 1992). Shor defines generative themes as "provocative themes discovered as unresolved social problems in the community, good for generating discussion in class on the relation of personal life to larger issues" (Shor, 1992, p. 47) Shor calls them "student-centered foundations for problem-posing" (Shor, 1992, p. 55). Freire called these themes generative because "they contain the possibility of unfolding into again as many themes, which in their turn call for new tasks to be fulfilled" (Freire, 1997, p. 83).

One important difference between our perspective on generative learning and previous uses of the term is that, in addition to focusing on individual learners, we expand our focus to multiple learners within nested and overlapping systems. These previous uses of the term, however, have contributed to our thinking, and we build on them, as well as on the research on complexity in general and our extensive work with colleagues in HSD. The work has led us to delineate five characteristics or features of generative teaching and learning in complex systems:

- Emergent
- Adaptive
- Creative
- Dialogic
- Scaled

We suggest that these features of "generative teaching/learning" contribute to its potential to trigger deep transformations that can sustain learning communities, both small and large, even through treacherous and unpredictable times.

Emergent

Briefly, **emergence** refers to a shift that involves two or more aspects of a system, allowing each to influence the other(s) to generate something entirely new. The original ceases to exist as the new emerges. Emergence is a holistic process—disparate or distinct parts come together to form a unified whole and cannot, at some later point, be reduced to the parts again. We see emergence, complex adaptive systems, and self-organization as different terms pointing to the same phenomenon, and we use the terms interchangeably. Chapter 3 provides further explanation of emergence as it relates to the simple rule "Attend to the whole, part, and greater whole."

Emergence is clearly related to generative teaching/learning. New learnings emerge within, between, and among people and ideas as new understandings, dispositions, strategies, behaviors, etc. rise or self-organize from the interaction of multiple parts or agents. (See Figure 2.1 above.)

English/language arts teachers and researchers may be familiar with the concept of emergence in the transactional approach to literary experience (Rosenblatt, 1938/1968; 1994). According to Rosenblatt, a literary "transaction" happens when particular readers engage/transact with a particular text. The resulting new meaning or "poem" emerges from this transaction. The new meaning is different from previous understandings, and subsequent readings (transactions) trigger other unique meanings. Although Rosenblatt's work precedes the work related to complex systems, she was influenced by the early 20th century physicists who were exploring alternatives to a Newtonian view of the universe. In fact, in her choice of the term "transaction," she cites Dewey and Bentley's 1949 distinction between a mechanical "interaction" (a billiard ball hitting another and changing the direction or position of other balls) and an organic, emergent "transaction" in which the emergent whole is different from the sum of the parts (Dewey and Bentley, 1949; Rosenblatt, 1938). Rosenblatt is pointing to **emergence** in our literary experiences, and when we talk about generative teaching/learning, we are pointing to emergence in broader learning experiences.

It is critical for educators to remember that emergence means that learning is happening every moment, every day, in every part of the system, in every area of our lives—with or without our deliberate attention. Emergence is beyond anyone's control. Students, teachers, administrators, parents, board members—one and all—are continually learning. We may not be learning what is on the lesson plan or on the meeting agenda. We may not be learning what will prove useful in the long run, but we are always learning.

Emergence also means that teaching and learning are full of surprises. "Ah-ha moments" are evidence of emergence. The surprising insight from the student who never speaks up and the random question at the faculty meeting that triggers a deep conversation about racism in the community—both of these are evidence of emergence. The challenge is for leaders—both formal and informal leaders—to set conditions so that desirable and sustainable learning opportunities like this can emerge. Of course, these generative leaders will also be standing in inquiry, open to emerging insights that may shift their understandings.

Adaptive

Generative teacher/learners are attentive and sensitive to surprises, to new patterns in the system. They listen to others; they watch the system; and they consider which options might best fit system needs. As we explore complex systems, we have come to believe that systems don't adapt because particular objectives have been determined in advance, but because agents naturally shift to reduce tension in the system, to move toward balance or **coherence**. That coherence may involve particular goals or objectives that have been outlined ahead of time, but, when that happens, it's a happy coincidence. Merely stating a goal does not mean that we can control the system's progress in that direction. Although a set of goals may be written into the strategic plan and announced at stakeholder meetings, healthy systems adapt to changing conditions without regard for specific written goals. The process is adaptive, not deterministic.

As agents in the system, of course, we need to think about the patterns we ultimately want to see across the system (our goals) and continuously stand ready to reevaluate and refine our actions in response to changing conditions within and outside the system. Our responses shift the conditions as we continue to work toward those desired patterns. Because we are never sure what will happen, this commitment to thoughtful adaptation can be uncomfortable. It can also be disconcerting for those who expect their leaders to take a more definitive and authoritative approach.

Effective teachers know that adaptation is the name of the game. They know the curricular expectations, and they know about their students' needs. They develop long- and short-range instructional plans with those needs in mind, but they also stand ready to adapt those plans day by day and, sometimes, moment by moment as they assess students' emerging responses. Schön called this adaptive process "reflection-in-action" (1991). Of course, this adaptive aspect of generative teaching/learning is also important for everyone in the system, including effective administrators, as they plan staff meetings and district-wide initiatives.

As teachers, when we take action according to what we think the system needs (or what our students need), we essentially shift the structures or processes within the teaching/learning system. That change (we hope) sets the **conditions** for learners to respond in appropriate ways to our instruction. (See Chapter 4 for a more thorough discussion of how to set these conditions.) When we do this, we are betting that a more or less persistent change in students' understandings and behavior will follow. The learner may initiate changes of her own—which, in turn will shift the system again. And—if we are teaching and learning in every interaction—we will be open to surprises and new learning. These cycles of adaptation and shifts in the system are what we mean when we say that generative teaching and learning are adaptive.

Adaptation happens both individually and collectively. As a teacher/learner, you and I can adapt together as long as we are both sensitive to patterns in our system(s) and responsive to one another. Our roles as teacher and learner are interchangeable and not necessarily related to the official position of a person in the system. We can all learn; we can all teach. When teacher/learners within a system adapt simultaneously in response to one another, we call that "**co-evolution.**" The longer I work in collaboration with a person, the more I/we teach, learn, and adapt to one another and to changing patterns in our shared systems. We co-evolve; our patterns become more similar over time. Our individual patterns contribute to a collective pattern.

To sustain a healthy complex system, this co-evolution must move toward **coherence**, or a balance among similarities and differences, across the system. For instance, from the first day of school, teachers can see connections and relationships emerging in their classrooms as the students learn how to respond productively to each other, to the teacher's style, and to the school's expectations. Across the classroom system, tension is released as difference is reduced and coherence builds.

On the other hand, collectively, if we self-organize in ways that manifest more difference or tension (in other words, if we do not co-evolve), we may experience so much dissension or turbulence that the system will split, and the original system will cease to exist. In classrooms we see this happen when kids totally "check out" without dropping out. Another example is when we see faculty groups split into cliques so that they have difficulty coming to shared agreements or engaging in collaborative work. Generative teaching/learning is adaptive and can help the system avoid those schisms.

Creative

Generative teaching/learning is creative because it opens the possibility for new patterns in the system. The patterns that emerge from this teaching/learning dynamic are often new and different from what came before. Of course, that brings some level of risk because the future may be neither familiar nor predictable. We go into teaching/learning situations without knowing precisely what we want to know or what we want to do differently. We can't know what patterns will emerge. And if we think we know what to expect, we are often surprised by what actually emerges. But with this risk comes the possibility that our most urgent questions will be answered and our stickiest issues will be resolved. Risk-taking is part of the price of creative teaching and learning.

We are not talking about "creativity" in the sense of composing music or inventing a new tool (although those are certainly desirable and involve the emergence of new patterns). We are talking about creativity in all our decisions, creativity that leads us to multiple perspectives and new possibilities, even in our most routine actions. We are talking not only about thinking outside the box but stacking the old boxes together in new and surprising ways. We need to remember that we always have the potential to create new patterns, even when we are doing relatively simple tasks or practicing rote skills.

Dialogic

We point to dialogic relationships as another feature of generative teaching/learning because we want to emphasize the need for democratic relationships, shared power, and open communication among administrators, teachers, parents, and students. These multiple and diverse voices can enrich our potentials for learning. The open give-and-take of dialogic learning essentially points to "**generative engagement**," which will be further explored in Chapter 5. **Generative Engagement** is a model that helps us consider and influence the interdependence of shared identity, shared power, and shared voice for each person in the system. In a classroom, this kind of engagement is the goal of generative learning as teachers invite students to make choices, to voice their opinions, and to use the knowledge they bring from their home cultures. At the campus level, generative leaders ensure that decision-making is transparent and that everyone has an opportunity to contribute their expertise to collective action. At the district level, leaders make it possible for all stakeholders to provide input and seek information.

An emphasis on dialogic learning is not original with human systems dynamics. Certainly, our emphasis on the necessity for dialogic teaching/learning owes a debt to a number of influential social theorists and researchers who have written about dialogic teaching and learning without explicit references to complexity science. Most notably, dialogic teaching/learning links to Freire's theory of dialogic action (1970), Habermas's theory of communicative action (1985, 1987), and Bakhtin's notion of dialogic imagination (1982). In adult learning theory, it resonates with Mezirow's transformative learning theory (2000) and Vella's dialogue education (2007).

In the arena of K-12 education, Wells's approach to dialogic inquiry (1999) is similar to the work of many researchers who advocate the use of both inquiry and dialogue (spoken, written, and other sign systems) to support and facilitate student learning (for example Lindfors, 1999; Short and Harste, 1996). Johnston's *Choice Words* (2004) and *Opening Minds* (2012) do not use the term "dialogic," but both books offer compelling arguments about the power of teacher talk to frame student agency, identity, and learning frames.

Fullan (2010) argues that dialogic teaching and learning build collective capacity and support whole system reform. As an example, he describes how an elementary teacher and her colleague participate in a buddy-day strategy implemented by the district and her principal:

> Every grade-level primary teacher (Grades 1-3) is buddied with a teacher at the junior level (Grades 4-6). The two buddied teachers plan the buddy-day monthly activities together. This allows the teachers to plan a two-day activity. One day, the junior teacher would be supervising the whole group; the next day the primary teacher would be overseeing the group as they complete the activity. Older children have the opportunity to explain and lead the activity with their younger buddies. . . The activities developed are kept in a binder for wider sharing and reference about hands-on teaching with mixed age groupings. (p. 7)

Generative teaching and learning are dialogic and reciprocal; teachers learn, and learners teach. Teaching and learning become collective experiences, a two-way holistic and organic process. Only in dialogic relationships like these can we live out the simple rule that is the focus of this chapter: Teach and learn in every interaction.

Scaled

Generative teaching/learning can "scale." In other words, it happens across layers or levels of the system. Chapter 3 will explain more bout how this happens, but the important point here is that, in a complex adaptive system, we see patterns, like generative learning, at all levels (or layers or scales) of the system. We think of the whole, the part, and the greater whole as "scales" of the system. If the classroom is the "whole," a single student is a "part" and the campus community is "the greater whole."

Where you stand in the system will determine your perspective about what is "whole, part, and greater whole." If generative learning scales across a particular system, we might see everyone taking an inquiry stance--tenth graders in a science lab; teachers at a faculty meeting; and school board members in a budget meeting. In other words, generative behaviors can "spread" across a system—horizontally and vertically. This point is so important that it has its own simple rule: Pay attention to the whole, the part, and the greater whole. That rule is the focus of Chapter 3.

These layers influence one another, so we sometimes say they are "massively entangled." A complex view of schools attends to simultaneous and ever-emerging dynamics among these many parts of the larger system—parts that overlap, nest one inside another, and layer one over another. Within these interdependent relationships, systemic patterns arise, disappear, and sustain.

In school systems, one way to think about multiple scales is to think of the individual learner, the classroom, the campus, the district, and the community. But when we "freeze" systems to talk about the dynamics at each of these scales, we risk forgetting that these agents also share membership in soccer teams, faith communities, neighborhoods, language groups, ethnicities, families, etc. It's important to remember that there is not one correct way to view these interdependent levels or scales of the system. Another way to say this is that the influence among the levels or scales is not necessarily linear or hierarchical. The power, influence, and interdependence do not necessarily flow from the "top-down" nor from the "bottom-up." In fact, these massively entangled systems are described as "scale-free" (Barabasi, 2002) By that, they mean that "scale" is inherent in the observer's perspective, not in the system itself. Looking at the system from one perspective, you see a particular pattern across particular scales, and you can see how the influence flows. From another perspective the same system might look quite different, with different scales being significant and different interactions becoming apparent. The most important point is that, because of this interdependence, what happens at one scale has the potential for influence across the system.

For example, from a parent's perspective, the relevant scale on a campus might focus on the classes to which their children are assigned: science, English, math, social studies, physical education, art, music, and so forth. From this perspective, the "part" is the student, and the "greater whole" his or her total academic experience. From an administrator's perspective, the relevant scales might be the classroom, grade level team, campus leadership team, campus administrative team, superintendent's cabinet, and the school board. From a third grade student's perspective, the relevant scales might be self, best friends, and the whole third grade. Generative leaders try to remember that all these scales are mutually influential and that particular perspectives are pertinent when considering particular issues. The goal is to look for potential influences across the system and to focus on the scale or scales that are most relevant to the challenge at hand.

So when we talk about scale, we don't want to forget all those relevant systems that influence the organizational levels in the school system. In generative teaching/learning, what happens at each scale has the potential for influencing the other scales. If you want to change things at one scale, you can sometimes try to shift conditions at the scale above or below. For example, if a principal wants to see more collaborative planning among teachers, she might provide time for collaboration in the school day, or she might provide a task (like preparing a presentation about their hands-on science activities to the parent organization) that gives teachers an authentic reason to collaborate. Those actions set conditions for systemic patterned change, and they are much more promising than simply telling the teachers, "Collaborate, or else!"

As agents in teaching/learning systems, we need to remember that any action we take can trigger "ripples" or "resonance" through multiple scales of the system. Because of the unpredictable, nonlinear dynamics within the system(s), that action may be amplified and modified as it moves through the scales. That gives us the potential for a "butterfly effect"—when small changes in one part of the complex system trigger large effects across the whole. In generative teaching/learning, you can observe the potential power of a single comment or a raised eyebrow. Because generative teaching/learning is scaled, teachers and learners need to be conscious of this potential for small actions having unimagined (or unimaginable) consequences. And this is true whether those teachers and learners are in the classroom, in the central office, at home, in the community, or in the boardroom.

Talking about "scales" in generative teaching and learning reminds us of these multiple nested and overlapping systems within the ✓ larger system. It also reminds us that even individuals and small groups hold the potential for sending ripples of influence throughout the entire system.

Examples of Generative Teaching and Learning

We have described five features of generative teaching/learning: **emergence, adaptation, creativity, dialogue, and scaling**. How do these features show up in schools? Of course, each context is unique, but here are comments from two HSD educators that suggest a couple examples of generative teaching/learning:

As a principal, my goal last year was to focus more on instruction than on non-instructional issues. So I began leaving my office and spending more time in classrooms, and that made a huge shift. It made a difference in my exchanges with the teachers. I mean, I found when I'm in the office all of the conversation is around the kids who are having trouble. When I'm in the classrooms, it's around what the lesson was and what the kids learned. And so that alone has shifted the conversation because when I'm on my way back from a classroom and I run into the teacher I saw earlier, suddenly our conversation is all about what I just saw in her room, what did I think, and around the instructional situation. I learned more about what was actually going on in the classrooms, and teachers learned more about me and my expectations for the students. And that has been great . . .

–Elementary principal

In my classroom, we were having a problem with partner talking so I sat with the class, and I asked them questions about a bunch of things that were happening—patterns they saw. What are we noticing? OK, so it's a pattern of a lack of respect for your partner. So how can we change that? And my students came up with a few things that they wanted to try and change. Since then it's been pretty good. We still have to go back and remind ourselves, but it's been pretty good.

—Elementary teacher

Both of these examples illustrate how new insights **emerged** as these professionals **adapted** to new information and changing situations. These professionals approached the situations with openness and **creativity**, and they engaged in **dialogue**. These reports from a principal and a classroom teacher suggest how this inquiry stance can spread, or **scale**, up and down and across a complex system.

WHAT IS ADAPTIVE ACTION?

Now that we have fully described "generative teaching and learning," we can look more deeply at the process, focusing on details about how this process happens. Such an explanation will help us think about how we can take thoughtful and deliberate action to shift teaching and learning patterns in schools.

Learning happens whether we think about it or not. When we engage with the world, we learn. Learning emerges from our experiences. In schools and other educational settings, however, much of our learning is conscious and deliberate. And, of course, when we talk about "teaching" we are surely talking about deliberate planning and action. So, from an HSD perspective, how do we intentionally teach and learn? The question is this:

> How do we make such a complex, emergent, and natural part of human life explicit and deliberate enough to maximize the possibility that it will happen in schools?

Another way to ask this question is

> How do we see, understand, and influence patterns in our systems?"

We have found that **Adaptive Action**—a deceptively simple inquiry/action cycle—can help us do just that.

Adaptive Action

As always in HSD, we try to focus on the underlying dynamics of the system. Those dynamics in generative teaching and learning refer to three overlapping and interdependent steps or phases of the process:

- Seeing patterns
- Understanding patterns; and
- Influencing patterns.

HSD frames these three phases as questions:

- What?
- So what?
- Now what?

First, we examine data (our experiences, objective data, published texts) to identify patterns (*What?*). Our description of these patterns leads us to consider what those patterns mean and to generate options for action (*So what?*). The actions (*Now what?*) we take then trigger subsequent cycles. What were the results of that action? So what do those results mean? Now what shall we do next? Now what are our new questions and concerns?

We call this inquiry/action cycle **Adaptive Action**. Adaptive Action is an iterative cycle that integrates inquiry with action at each step. It is not about conducting a long-term inquiry before taking action; nor is it a series of action steps before a summative evaluation. It is about continuous inquiry and adaption.

We developed this model to help people think and work in complex adaptive systems. It has worked for us and for others in many different settings—businesses, government agencies, families, schools, and communities. We think it works because it makes the generative teaching and learning process explicit and accessible. As agents or participants in the system, the more we understand about what is happening, the more likely it is that we can identify options for action that can set the conditions for patterns we want to see. And the more we watch the system closely, the more we are learning. This model is an organic integration of thought and action. We learn more about the world at the same time we are learning to act on and in the world. (See figure 2.2)

Glenda and Royce further explore Adaptive Action and provide examples from multiple arenas in *Adaptive Action: Leveraging Uncertainty in Your Organization* (2013). The most crucial contribution of Adaptive Action is that, if multiple people, throughout a system, consistently engage in Adaptive Action, the system is more flexible, responsive, and adaptive. In other words, we say that Adaptive Action helps the system build adaptive capacity. In schools, we see powerful opportunities for Adaptive Action among students, teachers, parents, administrators, non-instructional staff, school board members, and community-based stakeholders.

Figure 2.2: The Adaptive ActionCycle. This represents the three foundational questions that frame teaching and learning (inquiry-based thought and action) in human systems.

Here are some questions that people might ask at each point in the cycle:

What?
- What is happening?
- What am I experiencing?
- How am I feeling about those experiences?
- What did I expect?
- What surprises me?
- What are the similarities, differences, and connections I observe right now?

So What?
- So what do those experiences mean?
- So what are the significant patterns?
- So what patterns might various participants notice?
- So what conditions in the system give rise to those patterns?
- So what assumptions or ideologies might be at work to create those patterns?
- So what priorities might have created those patterns?
- So what communication exchanges might have influenced those patterns?
- So what might have come before?
- So what might come later?
- So what can I do to shift the patterns toward what I want them to be?
- So what actions might I take to change my patterns?

Now What?

- Now what are my new insights?
- Now what are my new questions?
- Now what shall I do differently?
- Now what will I do to collect data for the next cycle?
- Now what do others need to know about my Adaptive Action?

Research Connections

Educational theorists have long pointed to inquiry as the foundation of thinking and learning (for example, Dewey, 1938; Smith, 1975, 1998). This foundational inquiry cycle embedded in Adaptive Action is familiar to practitioners and researchers alike, although it may be labeled differently. (See Table 2.1 for a few representative examples.)

Table 2.1: Applications of Inquiry-based Approaches in Schools

FOCUS OF INQUIRY-BASED APPROACHES	EXAMPLES OF RESEARCHERS & THEORISTS
Instruction	Burke, 2010 Berghoff, Egawa, Harste, and Hoonan, 2000 Shor, 1992 Stringer, Christensen, and Baldwin, 2009 Wilhelm, 2007
Language Development	Genishi and Dyson, 2009 Johnston, 2004 Lindfors, 1999 Wells, 1999
Practitioner Action Research	Stringer, 2007 Anderson, 2007
Reflective Teaching	Phillips and Karr, 2010 Schön, 1991 Zeichner and Liston, 1996
Coaching and Mentoring	Burley and Pomphrey, 2011 Costa and Garmston, 2002

Connections to Other School Improvement Cycles

Similar cycles are widely used in school reform efforts, especially among teams of teachers, as in professional learning communities. One of these cycles—Plan, Do, Check, Act (PDCA) or the Deming Cycle— became popular in the 1980s in management circles (Deming, 1986). This cycle is familiar to many educators as the basis for examining test data to adjust instructional practices for continuous improvement. Although the similarity to Adaptive Action is obvious, the differences are critical, and they have much to do with the flexibility inherent in Adaptive Action. (See Table 2.2 for similarities and differences between Adaptive Action and other such cycles.)

First, the three central prompts are questions—not directives or imperatives. Questions, of course, open potentials for meaning making and are applicable to a wide range of contexts or concerns. Adaptive Action can trigger and support authentic inquiry of any kind, in any context. Kindergartners can use it to explore how caterpillars turn into butterflies:

- What is happening? What are these caterpillars doing?
- So what might that mean? What made them do that? What might happen next?
- Now what are my new questions? Now what shall we do to record what we are learning?

Twelfth graders can use it to analyze a Shakespearean sonnet:

- What are the literal meanings of the words and phrases?
- So what are other possible meanings of these words or phrases? So how does the poem make me feel? So what am I reminded of? So how did Shakespeare use language to trigger my response as a reader?
- Now what have I learned that I can use when I read another poem? Or when I write a poem myself?

Second, Adaptive Action is different from most other school improvement cycles because the "So what?" question can trigger a deep, critical exploration of the conditions that trigger self-organization. This can result in an explanation, not just a description of the phenomenon. We have found that explanation leads directly into action—it is an actionable way to understand the patterns we study. Explanations can address issues like these: the underlying dynamics, cultural and political ideologies, economic constraints, and multiple interpretations. In contrast, the models like Plan-Do-Check-Act usually assume a fairly narrow focus on action and results—continuous improvement related to one task or a single function within the organization. Adaptive Action can be used in that way, of course, for example, for a particular instructional objective like "How can we improve writing fluency among our fifth graders?" Adaptive Action can also be used for broader and more open-ended questions related to an organization's vision or identity like "Who are we and what do we want to accomplish in the next five years?" And, Adaptive Action can be used to address relationships among people.

- What behaviors do I notice (in myself or others)?
- So what is the result of those behaviors? So what is my story about those behaviors? So how do others interpret my behavior? So what conditions might be influencing these behaviors?

- Now what shall I do to change this relationship?

Table 2.2: Similarities and Differences between Adaptive Action and Other Inquiry/Action Cycles

SIMILARITIES	DIFFERENCES
• Adaptive Action and other inquiry/action cycles, like PDCA and PDSA, support practitioners to describe and examine what is happening—the status quo. • The goal of all these approaches is to generate options for action.	• Adaptive Action is essentially an inquiry, (framed by questions) rather than directives, like Plan, Do, Study, Act (which seem to imply that the recommended actions will be apparent and unambiguous). • Adaptive Action can be adapted for all audiences and all situations (with young children and adults, in games and at work). • Adaptive Action includes the "So What?" question, an open-ended question that triggers interpretation and inference about larger issues and theoretical concerns. • Adaptive Action can be used with a narrow focus on a particular technical problem, or it can be used to address more abstract and long-term challenges. • Adaptive Action is flexible enough to use with both well-defined technical problems and with "messy" human problems. • Adaptive Action leads naturally from one iteration into the next; the "Now What?" step invites us to describe what happened in the next iteration of "What?" It becomes internalized as "standing in inquiry," no matter the context. Because it informs action at the next level, you never get stuck.

Finally, although other inquiry cycles can, of course, be repeated with positive effects, HSD practitioners tell us that Adaptive Action leads seamlessly from one cycle into another and another, even to the point at which it is hard to tell where one cycle begins and another ends. (And that really doesn't matter.) The "Now What?"—new actions or new questions—leads immediately into a new "What?" And this iterative cycle can fairly quickly become integral to the culture of a classroom or campus or district—so that everyone in the system is engaging in Adaptive Action without really thinking about it as a separate tool or method. Here is evidence of that from a literacy coach on an elementary campus:

> *I've been trying to get at the heart of the teachers' concerns by asking lots of questions . . . It's really been about asking questions and not jumping to conclusions. I've really been working on trying to listen. I'm asking them what makes them feel that way? Where is that coming from? What is the evidence that's led you to believe this or hold this belief? And really, it actually, has had a big impact.*

There's actually one teacher in our school who has, until recently, always caused tension in staff meetings. I've tried to work with this person for five years, and it never went well. And the frustration with this person was building across the campus. So this year, I really took on that person with Adaptive Action, and we have developed a great relationship now. It was just about us having conversations—him growing as a teacher and me growing as a coach and helping the students grow as learners. We got down to some really foundational things that he was thinking and feeling. That work we've been doing all year has now affected and influenced his relationship with his grade-level team. That was always a difficult group, but now that team has actually asked me to come in and plan with them. They say my work with him has helped the grade-level planning meetings tremendously. And then it's affected the campus staff meetings because we can keep moving and more people have a voice. This person's not dominating or taking the discussion off track. So that's just one example. Like it started so small with one person but it's really had tremendous effects across the site, and people are coming to me, asking for help all the time now. The only difference I can see is that I used Adaptive Action.

–Literacy coach on an elementary campus

In schools, Adaptive Action cycles are powerful, no matter who you are or what your role is in the system. Obviously, administrators can use these three questions to lead long-range planning. Teams of teachers can use the cycle to set instructional priorities and to differentiate instruction. Students can use these questions as they read a textbook or a poem. Counselors can use Adaptive Action to address the persistent problem of disengaged students. It is useful for individuals, for small groups and for whole faculties. It is useful in classrooms, in policy meetings, on the playground, and in the rehearsal hall.

In short, human systems dynamics practitioners see Adaptive Action as the primary method/model for working in complex adaptive systems. Adaptive Action first helps us see the relevant patterns and then helps us decide how we might influence those patterns, given what we know about the dynamics of complex adaptive systems. We argue that Adaptive Action (this meaning-making-and-acting cycle) is what human complex adaptive systems naturally do to survive and thrive—at the individual, group, and cultural scales. This meaning-making-and-acting cycle we have labeled Adaptive Action is common to all human beings. It is sometimes conscious and deliberate, but, often, it works without our conscious attention. It is the process that makes adaptation possible, and, it is, therefore, what makes life (and teaching/learning) sustainable in our ever-changing, always challenging environment.

Adaptive Action is especially appropriate for the complex and nonlinear nature of generative teaching and learning. Here are some reasons we think it works, especially in complex educational settings to create that space of generative learning:

- The cycle is framed as questions, to help teacher/learners stand in inquiry, which allows them to explore possibilities.

- The language is common, simple, and accessible to anyone, which means learners at all levels can learn from one other.

- The questions are useful at every scale, in any context of human systems—individuals, classrooms, buildings, districts, boards, communities--so learners can explore their world with open questions about relationships, dependencies, connections.

- The "So What?" question requires some degree of critique, encouraging participants to think about larger system patterns and constraints. With this step the inquiry can take a critical turn.

- All agents/participants can be held accountable for engaging in the cycle--it's not just for those designated as leaders in the system.

- These questions focus on the underlying conditions of self-organizing systems—requiring participants to notice and name emergent patterns, always with the goal of generating options for action (see Chapter 4 for a more thorough discussion of these conditions).

- These questions assume the integration of thought and action, theory and practice--the essence of generative teaching/learning.

- Simple, elegant, powerful—Adaptive Action, when implemented throughout a system, sets conditions for adaptive learning that is inquiry based, locally determined, focused on fit and coherence, infinitely variable, based on and responsive to diversity, AND simple.

Adaptive Action moves us beyond controversy about whether change should begin at the top or at the bottom. With Adaptive Action, change can begin everywhere in the system at once. As everyone makes their discoveries public and as dialogue shapes shared questions and shared goals, the collective effect of multiple Adaptive Actions will, without a doubt, shift the system. Through subsequent Adaptive Action, agents can decide whether that shift is useful. Whatever they decide will shape their next Adaptive Action.

In addition, and perhaps even more important, Adaptive Action helps us focus on what "fits" the system—what "works" or what helps the system "adapt" in responsive ways. Remember that Adaptive Action is how we do generative teaching/learning. That integration of teaching and learning means the official "teacher" takes an inquiry stance, expecting to learn from the Adaptive Action. And the official "student" has agency and can take their own Adaptive Action to make decisions about what they need to learn and how.

What Does the Learner's Landscape Tell Us about Instruction as Adaptive Action?

Given that flexibility, we do not need to make long-term commitments to a single answer, approach, method or program. Teachers can take small actions and then adjust based on new patterns they see. They can then repeat that process again and again as they note how the patterns shift. For that reason, Adaptive Action can move beyond divisive dichotomies about the "right" instructional method—structured versus unstructured; student-centered versus teacher-directed; hands-on versus text-based. These are truly false dichotomies. Thoughtful teachers know that occasionally learners need (or the task calls for) one extreme or the other, but usually wise teachers know that the appropriate choice for learners somehow combines or balances these extremes. Repeated iterations of Adaptive Action can help find the optimal support that fit the conditions in a particular day or week for a particular student or group.

In short, although Adaptive Action is essentially an open-ended, inquiry-based approach to decision making in schools, it can support a wide variety of educational philosophies and instructional approaches, including more convergent and predictable teaching methods. Teachers who use Adaptive Action as an instructional model would ask questions like these:

- **What** do my students currently know? What can they do?
- **What** are the curricular objectives?
- **What** are my constraints in terms of time, materials, etc.?
- **What** are the students' interests? their cultural backgrounds? their linguistic proficiencies?
- **So what** is the impact of their interests? cultural backgrounds? linguistic proficiencies?

- **So what** are the connections that hold this class and these ideas together?
- **So what's** important to these students in this particular experience?
- **So what** would most likely engage this group of students in the required content?
- **So what** guiding questions would trigger their interest and link to the core concepts and skills to be learned?
- **Now what** learning experiences are most likely to engage these students and provide the support they need?
- **Now what** will I look for to know what students are learning and to what degree?
- **Now what** assessment tools or methods will best provide information about what the students are learning?

Time Out for Reflection

How can I support myself and others in using Adaptive Action in intentional and focused ways to increase learning and insights?

Because collaborative Adaptive Action assumes that students have agency and are invited into dialogue about the content and also about the teaching/learning process, teachers can listen to student input as they adjust and adapt, providing more structure when necessary and encouraging more student independence when possible.

The Learner's Landscape Diagram (Figure 2.3) suggests how Adaptive Action can help a learner (and teacher) make appropriate choices among a range of instructional practices. Think of the diagram as representing two dimensions of the teaching/learning situation. One dimension is about whether or not the learning task in convergent (one or a few "right" responses) or divergent (many "right" responses). The other dimension is about whether or not the learning is predictable and familiar. If the learning is highly predictable and converges on one right answer, then the learning task is about internalizing that answer, which may require drill, practice, and memorization. At the other extreme, if the learning is not at all predictable and if there are many possible "answers," a high degree of openness and creativity is appropriate. Often, the optimal learning happens somewhere on this landscape between those extremes.

The learner can use Adaptive Action (What? So What? Now What?) at each point on this landscape to practice skills or to explore a topic, but the three basic questions still apply. The teacher, on the other hand, also uses Adaptive Action to assess what the student needs, to choose appropriate instructional methods, and to evaluate student learning.

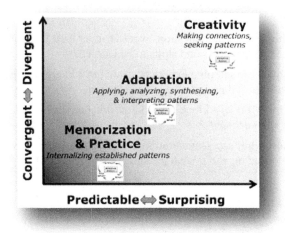

Figure 2.3: Learner's Landscape. This model, modified from the Landscape Diagram (Eoyang and Holladay, 2013) and in Chapter 3, helps teachers use Adaptive Action to make decisions about what kind of learning experience is appropriate for particular tasks and students.

Adaptive Action builds individual and system capacity to fit each instructional decision to particular learner profiles and immediate observations, to decide which instructional approach fits in a given circumstance, and to guide generative inquiry/action cycles that help the system move toward coherence. Here are a few examples of instructional objectives that fit each area of the Learner's Landscape:

- Bottom-Left: Adaptive Action to Internalize Established Patterns—Memorization and Practice
  - Memorize math facts
  - Learn Greek and Latin roots of English words
  - Memorize and use the periodic table of elements
  - Memorize the states and capitals
- Middle: Adaptive Action to Apply, Analyze, Synthesize, and Interpret Patterns
  - Summarize informational text

- Find themes in literature
- Create timelines
- Conduct and report on chemistry lab activities
- Solve word problems
- Participate in a debate

- Top-Right: Adaptive Action to make connections or seek patterns
  - Create a blog
  - Compose a poem
  - Develop a metaphor or analogy
  - Create a personal response to a response or prompt

THE ROLE OF LANGUAGE AND OTHER SIGN SYSTEMS

In Adaptive Action, we use language and other sign systems to respond to all three basic questions. First, we use symbols and signs to name the patterns we notice (with words/labels, illustrations, charts, music, and gestures). Second, we interpret the meanings of these emergent patterns by generating and using symbolic tools (lists, stories, metaphors, charts, rubrics, equations, visual representations, etc.) Finally, we use these multiple sign systems to help us take action—to mediate, represent, and support our own meaning making and to work with others to build shared understandings and to take social action. This role of sign systems in Adaptive Action is critical. Vygotsky and the socio-cultural researchers who followed him call that symbolic support "mediation." This use of symbols to mediate generative teaching and learning is critical to our work in human systems dynamics, and we have learned a great deal from sociocultural theorists and researchers about how this mediational process can work across diverse settings (see, for example, John-Steiner and Mahn, 1996; Lantolf, 2006; Vygotsky, 1986; Wells, 2007; 2009; Wertsch, 1991).

We have a great deal more to learn about those linguistic and other symbol systems and their role in human systems dynamics, but we know that we see examples of generative teachers and learners using these mediational tools in powerful ways. For example, as teachers are presenting new content, they generate anchor charts to list characteristics of the unfamiliar concepts. Textbooks and web resources represent both primary and secondary sources that can tell learners about the world. These anchor charts, textbooks, and websites are all mediational tools. As we put our learning into words (or pictures, etc.), to share our insights with others, we are, in fact, "teaching," even in informal conversations at the corner coffee shop. In those teaching moments, we work together to see, understand, and influence emerging patterns, and we use signs and symbols to help represent what we are learning. Those tools are critical to our Adaptive Actions, so we need to pay close attention to how language and other signs work in our complex adaptive systems.

What Are Teachers' and Learners' Roles?

Clearly everyone in generative teaching/learning systems are "adaptive actors"—active meaning makers and pattern influencers. The teacher/learner's role in generative learning is deceptively simple. No matter the particular task, Adaptive Action is the heart of the work. Individuals "simply" use Adaptive Action to see, understand, and influence patterns to move the system toward coherence. A deeper dive into those three Adaptive Action questions yields more specific recommendations for teachers and learners:

What?

- Stand in inquiry.
- Explore the external world.
- Reflect on what you already know.

So What?

- Notice puzzles, anomalies, questions, and dissonances.
- Look for patterns around those issues, etc.
- Gather more information about your issue of interest.
- Make sense or interpret patterns in the information or data.
- Think about relationships in those patterns (possible influences? possible implications?).
- Think about the conditions in the system that generated those patterns.

Now What?

- Use what you are learning to take action in and on the world.
- Share what you are learning.
- Ask new questions.
- Begin the process again.

Subsequent Cycles

- Assess whether and how you answered your original question.
- Pay attention to how the learning is going.

- Think about what you'll do or say differently next time.

As we discussed in the Introductory Note, people in school systems face profound challenges in public schools today, but, from an HSD perspective, the "prime directive" to all of us is to stand in inquiry, regardless of the task at hand.

Just imagine how that shift in both teaching and learning might set conditions for radical new patterns in schools.

So What about Student Engagement?

One of the major challenges for would-be school reformers today is how to sustain student interest and engagement in relevant learning tasks. Prensky says that student engagement is THE challenge facing educators. He makes a compelling argument that today's students say, "Engage me or enrage me" (2005, p. 60).

We argue that Adaptive Action, leading to generative teaching/learning is the only way to deeply engage our students. If students do not engage in teaching/learning experiences, they can't progress. If academic tasks are too challenging, students disengage because they lose hope. If tasks are too easy, students tune out because they are bored.

Time Out for Reflection
How does student engagement present a challenge to you and your colleagues? What have you found that works? How does that connect with your current understandings of generative teaching and learning? With Adaptive Action for students?

In response to this challenge, Jones, Valdez, Nowakowski, and Rasmussen (1994) developed "indicators of engaged learning." They recommend that these indicators be used as both a vision and a set of guidelines for school reform. We are struck by the coherence between these indicators and what we have described in this chapter as generative teaching/learning. When everyone in school (not just the students) continually asks "What?, So What? and Now What?" –we predict that everyone will ultimately see these as indicators of engaged learning become more pronounced:

Vision of Engaged Learning. Successful, engaged learners are responsible for their own learning, self-regulating, energized, and joyful. Engaged learning also involves collaboration.

Tasks for Engaged Learning. To invite engaged learning, tasks need to be challenging, authentic, and multidisciplinary.

Assessment of Engaged Learning. Assessment of engaged learning involves an authentic task, project, or investigation; assessing what students actually know and can do.

Instructional Models & Strategies for Engaged Learning. The most powerful models of instruction are interactive and generative. Instruction should encourage the learner to construct and produce knowledge in meaningful ways.

Learning Context of Engaged Learning. For engaged learning to happen, the classroom must be conceived of as a knowledge-building learning community.

Grouping for Engaged Learning. Collaborative work involves small, heterogeneous groups or teams of students.

Teacher Roles for Engaged Learning. The role of the teacher in the classroom has shifted from "information giver" to "facilitator, guide, and learner."

Student Roles for Engaged Learning. Engaged students are explorers and cognitive apprentices, and teachers. Apprenticeship takes place when students observe and apply the thinking processes used by practitioners. Students also become teachers themselves by integrating, using, and sharing what they've learned. (See http://www.ncrel.org/sdrs/engaged.htm)

As we said above, we think these indicators of engaged learning can describe what everyone in schools should be doing–not just the students. We are convinced that if all of us—students, teachers, administrators, parents, non-instructional staff, school board members--are engaged learners, we will almost surely see fewer problems with student engagement and motivation. Adaptive Action gives us a flexible and generative framework that invites and sustains engagement for all.

NOW WHAT? TEACH AND LEARN TO ENHANCE ADAPTIVE CAPACITY

In human systems dynamics, we see radical school transformation as an ongoing generative teaching/learning process among all agents in the system. By radical, we mean foundational and transformational. Adaptive Action is the method that helps people follow the simple rule that is the focus of this chapter:

Teach and learn in every interaction.

When individuals across the system sincerely commit themselves to inquiry, we see evidence of this simple rule at work. When a substantial number of people in the system consistently engage in Adaptive Action, both individually and collectively, the system shifts in surprising ways. This is what happened in New Haven Unified School District, where approximately 100 people began using Adaptive Action in their work. We conclude this chapter with the words of three of these New Haven educators:

> . . . the change in the way people in the district think and interact has been pretty dramatic . . . . I think that there's a lot more focus on what we're doing, how we're doing it and what impact and effect it's having. So everybody's talking about patterns. And although, initially, the Adaptive Action questions probably felt a little bit staged, I think it becomes real the more you use it and the more people understand it and embrace it.

> –District Administrator

> The one thing I always have going through my brain is "What? So what? Now what?" Like what's going on with my class right now? I even had it happen in the middle of a lesson where you just kind of feel the lesson isn't going where you wanted it to go so you ask "What's going on right now? So what can I do right now to change that?"

> —Elementary Teacher

> . . . the biggest component is reminding me to stand in inquiry at all times. When I face a conflict, if I can hold on to that—standing in inquiry—I feel like everything else will kind of take care of itself. Because it removes judgment; it removes people feeling that they're being evaluated; and it can diffuse the conflict and let you move forward. . . . For example, when we looked at our patterns around discipline on our campus, we began standing in inquiry.

> —Secondary Teacher

Whoever we are and wherever we work in the system—administrators, teachers, staff, students, family members, school board members, or patrons in the community—we can use Adaptive Action to work on our most pressing problems. Adaptive Action triggers inquiry into the emergent patterns that we notice in our systems. It helps us better understand the underlying dynamics. It moves us beyond merely describing our problems (creating taxonomies and lists of competencies or standards) and helps us hypothesize about the underlying conditions that influence these patterns.

As we engage in generative teaching/learning, we learn more; we teach one another; and our schools change in radical ways—if, every moment, every person stands in inquiry. The first simple rule—**Teach and learn in every interaction**—clearly sets conditions for radical change in schools and beyond.

NOW WHAT? USE THESE RESOURCES TO LEARN MORE

Committee on Increasing High School Students' Engagement and Motivation to Learn, National Research Council. (2003). *Engaging schools.* Washington, D.C.: *National Academies Press.* Retrieved January, 2013 from http://www.nap.edu/catalog/10421.html

Crowell, S. and Reid-Marr, D. (2013). *Emergent teaching: A path of creativity, significance, and transformation.* Lanham: Rowman & Littlefield Education.

Davis, B. & Sumara, D. (2006). *Complexity and education: Inquiries into learning, teaching, and research.* Mahweh, NJ: Lawrence Erlbaum Associates, Publishers.

Davis, B. & Sumara, D. (2007). Complexity science and education: Reconceptualizing the teacher's role in learning. *Interchange, 38 (1),* 53-67.

Digital Is, National Writing Project. http://digitalis.nwp.org/

Eckert, P., Goldman, S., & Wenger, E. (1993). The school as a community of engaged learners. Palo Alto, CA: *IRL* working paper. www.stanford.edu/~eckert/PDF/SasCEL.pdf

Eoyang, G. H. (2012). Sir Issac's dog: Learning for adaptive capacity. *The F. M. Duffy Reports, 17,* 2, 1-12.

Freire, P. & Macedo, D. (1998). *Pedagogy of freedom.* Lanham: Rowman & Littlefield Publishers, Inc.

Institute for Democracy, Education and Access (IDEA). http://idea.gseis.ucla.edu/

Johnston, P. (2012). *Opening minds: Using language to change lives.* Portland, ME: Stenhouse Publishers.

Jones, B., Valdez, G., Nowakowski, J., & Rasmussen, C. (1994). *Designing learning and technology for educational reform.* Oak Brook, IL: North Central Regional Educational Laboratory.

Jones, R. and Brown, D. (2011). The mentoring relationship as a complex adaptive system: Finding a model for our experience. *Mentoring & Tutoring: Partnership in Learning. 19,* 4, 401-418.

Prensky, M. (2005). Engage me or enrage me. What today's learners demand. *Educause Review, September/October, 2005,* pp. 60-64.

Schelchty, P. C. (2011). *Engaging students: The next level of working on the work.* San Francisco, CA: Jossey-Bass.

Wickstrom, C., Araujo, J., Patterson, L., and Hoki, C. (2011). Teachers prepare students for careers and college: "I see you," therefore I can teach you. *60th Yearbook of the Literacy Research Association.* Oak Creek, WI: Literacy Research Association, Inc.

Wickstrom, C., Patterson, L., and Isgitt, J. (2012). One teacher's implementation of Culturally Medited Writing Instruction. *61st Yearbook of the Literacy Research Association.* Oak Creek, WI: Literacy Research Association, Inc.

CHAPTER 3:
Whole, Part, and Greater Whole

Simple Rule:
Pay attention to patterns in the whole, part, and greater whole.

From a human systems dynamics perspective, teaching and learning focus on emergent patterns throughout the system. To understand how to work in these systems, we need to understand how patterns emerge across each scale in each system—in their parts and in the greater whole. This chapter explains how similar patterns emerge and can be sustained across the system.

Central Challenge	To ensure sustainability
Simple Rule	Pay attention to patterns in the whole, part, and greater whole.
Concepts, Methods, and Models	• Emergence • Coherence • Culture • Landscape Diagram • Constraints
Guiding Questions	• What is emergence? • How do tension and coherence contribute to emergence? • So what about coherence and culture? • So what shapes emergence and coherence? • So what about ensuring sustainability? • Now what? Enhance adaptive capacity throughout the system. • Now What? Use these resources to learn more.

A classroom is not just a collection of disparate students. A school is not just a common space for isolated and independent classrooms. A school district is not just a random accumulation of schools and organizational departments. A community is not a geographical location for disconnected individuals, families, businesses, and schools.

At each of those scales of the system, the parts interact with one other, creating a unique whole that carries out its work in specific ways. In Chapter 1, we explained how system-wide agreements about behavior (simple rules) generate patterns that come to characterize the whole. The classes in a school—even when the teachers shut their doors—are part of that whole. They serve all students who pass through multiple learning experiences across time. Each campus is comprised of multiple classes and departments. Each community is a system of interdependent families and neighborhoods, businesses and services, governance challenges, and cultures that create the whole. The health of the system, as a greater whole, depends on the degree to which the parts work together to contribute to the fitness or sustainability of the whole.

The good news is that in the last several years, school reformers have recognized the challenges inherent in those interconnections, interdependencies, and situated local needs. The not-so-good news is that, too often, formal reform efforts are blind to these connections. These efforts often treat the parts in isolation, ignoring the system-wide need for unity, coherence, and sustainability. When everyone throughout the system stands together in inquiry, each individual can better see the whole:

> *So what has happened with our policy teams across the district is that, instead of having a telescope, we have a microscope. We're focused in on our issues and what's happening at our site and our grade level, but we're not connected laterally to what other teams are doing at the same grade level. We're not connected to the middle school or the high school to understand what their issues are. And we're not connected to the district leadership. . . So, for example, we want to make a change to the report card. How is that going to affect the parents? The teachers? And how are we going to keep records and store the data? If we get people to represent the part, the whole and the greater whole all together, to give the policy makers a broader view of what it is they're trying to accomplish, that would help more people get their needs met rather than just a few.*
>
> *–Elementary Teacher*

As we emphasize throughout this book, "parts" of the school district come together in interdependent relationships we call complex adaptive systems (CAS), forming whole school systems that are, in fact,

56

parts of even greater systems at the state and federal levels. When we talk about the "layers" of relationships and interaction that we see in a system, we are really talking about "scale," as we described it in Chapter 2. In this chapter, we discuss how the whole of a system emerges from the interplay of the parts, and how these "wholes" are parts that come to define a greater whole. That leads us to the second simple rule:

Pay attention to patterns in the whole, part, and greater whole.

WHAT IS EMERGENCE?

As we explained in Chapter 2, emergence is a feature of generative teaching/learning and, therefore, an important concept when we think about self-organizing processes in schools. We use the term **emergence** as another term for self-organizing dynamics. Emergence happens when systems self-organize. Emergence describes the rise of something new from the interaction of multiple parts (or agents in human systems). The original conditions or agents are irreversibly changed through the interaction, and something new comes into being. This is true of generative teaching/learning: As we learn new facts and gain new perspectives, our old ideas are enhanced or enriched, but we cannot go back and "unlearn" what we now know.

It is true of generative relationships: When individuals come together in a unique team, each one maintains a separate identities. However, each individual is influenced and irreversibly changed by his or her experience on the team. That is true at all scales of a complex system. As parts self-organize, they form patterns of the whole, and although they retain their own individuality, they also are further influenced by the patterns in the larger system.

This is the process we represented in Chapter 1 and again in Figure 3.1The larger pattern **emerges**. The phenomenon of emergence can be seen at all scales of human systems. Human behavior at the individual, group, and community level manifests as patterns of interaction and decision-making. Relationship patterns emerge as friendships or rivalries. Family patterns emerge as roles and responsibilities. Cultural patterns emerge as traditions and rituals. Regional and national patterns emerge as social, economic, and political agreements and structures.

In a complex adaptive system, emergence of patterns at one scale is influenced by the similarities, differences, and connections (patterns) that occur at other scales of that same system. Patterns of behavior and performance in the classroom are influenced by the ways the teacher reinforces particular actions and ideas among the individual students. What is important at the district level—ideas, relationships, and behavioral

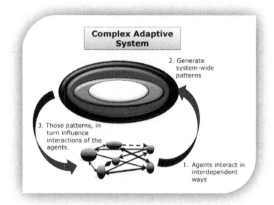

Figure 3.1: Emergent patterns in a complex adaptive system (CAS). Agents interact, which creates system-wide patterns that subsequently influence the agents' interactions.

expectations—influence the patterns that emerge at each of the campuses. Similarly the community's standards, culture, and expectations influence the overall patterns inside the school district.

In a highly diverse and open human system, such as a school district, multiple forces stand ready to influence patterns at all scales. Differences in politics, organizations, culture, language, and economics, for instance, can drive multiple patterns across the school district. We see this often in large, urban districts in response to the many constituencies they serve. Often these systems appear to be schizophrenic as they bounce from initiative to initiative; focusing on students, then schools, then communities; responding to local, state, and national requirements and mandates. In that case, emergent patterns often compete for resources and attention in the various parts, with no real coherence across the whole. The challenge for educators is to set conditions for emergence in similar ways so that the system can move toward coherence for all of the wholes, parts, and greater whole—whether that system is the individual learner, a classroom of learners, a school building or the whole district. Simple rules are one way to set those conditions for similarity.

How Do Coherence and Tension Contribute to Emergence?

Emergence in human systems is not under our control. It happens whether we know it or not, whether we like it or not, and whether we want it or not. In human systems dynamics, we say that self-organization is triggered, not by an intentional effort to move toward a particular pattern or goal, but by the system's inherent drive toward the reduction of **tension**, toward **coherence**—a balance among similarities and differences. As difference builds in a system, so does the tension. A system strives for such a balance as it moves to release the accumulating tension among differences in the system. In other words, a system strives toward "fitness"—toward an appropriate balance of similarities and differences. Coherence emerges as the system approaches that balance and as unnecessary tension is relieved.

We use the word "tension" as physicists use it, to refer to the potential energy that builds until it is released by a shift in system conditions. Something inside the system shifts; and the tension is relieved. For examples, earthquakes demonstrate what happens when energy builds up in the earth's crust. At some critical point, the tension exceeds the conditions that hold it, and it releases. The release of energy results in new conditions and apparent stability. In that shift, more coherent patterns emerge. In human systems, an example is when nervous laughter signals the release of tension in an emotionally stressful situation. The laughter relieves a bit of tension, and a more coherent (and comfortable) feeling emerges in the group.

This move toward fitness or coherence happens in schools, too. In schools, we typically think of tension as a negative—leading to avoidable or undesirable conflict. But we think of tension in a different way. Tension results from differences in a system. It is natural and neutral. It can lead to "bad" results, but it can also lead to desirable changes and positive effects, as in this story from an elementary school teacher:

> We've been creating a writing workshop unit and at first
> we just couldn't get anywhere. We just couldn't agree on
> anything. Finally we came to an understanding and
> agreement about what we want our students to leave with.
> Then we were able to work backwards and build from
> there. We all had the same idea of what students wanted
> to leave with, but we didn't have the same idea on how to
> get them there. We realized we didn't have to get all
> students to the same place in the same ways. What we
> needed was to be sure they left with the same tools and
> just as empowered as everyone in that grade level. That's
> how I came to understand that we needed "coherence"
> across our grade level more than we needed one set of
> instructional strategies.
>
> —Writing Teacher

Characteristics that Signal Coherence

In her analysis of self-organization in human systems (Eoyang, 2002), Glenda identified seven characteristics that signal coherence—the optimal (and dynamical) state of a vital and sustainable human system:

- Shared goals
- Reduction of tension
- Complementary functions
- Shared meaning
- Ability to adapt internally and externally
- Repeated patterns
- Sustainable and non-redundant use of energy

In HSD, this is how we identify coherent patterns. As systems self-organize, these characteristics emerge from the interactions among the agents. It is important to repeat that coherence is not about the absence of difference or tension—both are essential to the ongoing nonlinear work of the system as it responds and adapts. Coherence is about an appropriate balance along a continuum from dysfunctional redundancy and sameness to dysfunctional randomness and difference.

Further, coherence is not static; the system is never at rest in a "coherent place." Change is continual and inexorable. Coherence emerges continuously as the system adapts each moment along the continuum to reduce tension and settle into its own optimal balance. Think of the myriad, tiny adjustments that a gymnast makes as she performs on a balance beam. That kind of balance-in-motion is a metaphor for the system coherence we are describing.

When we apply this to a classroom, we can think of a continuum from random behavior to complete standardization. At one end of the continuum, every student randomly does his or her own thing; at the other end, all students are working in a lock-step manner. Neither would be productive over time, and there is no one place that is the exactly right amount of random or sameness. The appropriate balance depends on the context. In a fire drill, you want all the students to respond in a similar and predictable way. In a creative writing workshop, however, you want students to pursue their own ideas, but in a more or less orderly way. What you seek is coherence. Are all the students working toward similar goals with the least amount of energy wasted? . . . with the least possible tension in the system? . . . helping and supporting each other in positive and productive ways? . . . adapting to what new challenges? . . . cooperating with their classmates? That is coherence at one scale. For the moment, let's call the classroom scale the "whole."

At the same time the whole class is engaging in a given activity—say a fire drill—how is each individual responding? Is this student doing what he or she is supposed to be doing? Is this child overly frightened? . . . taking the practice seriously? . . . knowing what to do? Is that child being able to adapt to what's going on each moment? That's coherence at another scale. Let's call that the "part."

Even as a teacher is dealing with and supporting the many individual students (parts) to bring the class (whole) to safety in the fire drill, all classes and staff in the building are also moving together, responding to needs, taking Adaptive Actions in the moment to be sure that the building accomplishes this task in an acceptable way. Classes go where they are supposed to go. Each one checks in as he and she is told. Stragglers are helped to find their ways. That's coherence at a larger scale. Let's call that the "greater whole."

So even as individuals engage in any kind of activity in the school--learning, performing, playing, following rules--they are also a part of the multiple scales across the school. In the same way, the school is a part of the greater whole of the district. The district is a part of the greater whole of the community and the statewide or national educational system. When similarities and differences across these scales is balanced, the system is coherent.

Emergence of Coherent Patterns: An Example

Here is an example. Say that two teachers who work in side-by-side classrooms have different styles of teaching. One is highly ordered and maintains strict behavioral standards. Coherence in that classroom emerges as students learn to interact in ways that meet her expectations. Often without even realizing it, the students develop shared goals and practices. Tension is relieved as students learn to fit in. They help each other know the rules. Children know how to act in this classroom and among their fellow students at recess. Each day is much like the one before; and as the rules become clear, it takes little energy to enforce them. The system becomes internally coherent, perhaps without the conscious awareness or intention of either the classmates or teacher.

Next door, the teacher believes that learning is noisy and messy. Students are encouraged to engage in independent research, lively debate, and artistic expression of their own ideas in the context of the new learning. This class also develops internal coherence as students learn the rules, help each other align with expectations and move forward together.

In this case, as well, coherence emerges, perhaps without the teacher's conscious awareness or intention. These coherent patterns are, however, different from what emerges next door.

Those two parts of the system are each internally coherent, but when the two classes come together to work on the winter holiday program, their cultures clash and tension builds. The internal coherence of each is threatened as this greater whole comes to terms with the two different sets of rules. As the teachers and students work out particular points of disagreement, the two teachers figure out how their expectations are similar, different, and complementary. At the same time, the students find a new level of coherence as they figure out which rules fit in which situations and how to work out tensions within and between themselves.

The key to this movement toward coherence is that these two teachers acknowledge and resolve tensions to support student learning, and they recognize that the tension they experienced was a natural part of a self-organizing process. Schlechty (2009) points out that, because most educators don't understand these social systems,

> . . . they are apt to view the tensions or conflicts resulting from an innovation as evidence that the change will not work in their school. The result is that innovations are adopted and abandoned for reasons that have little to do with their potential benefit to children. Rather, they are adopted and abandoned on the basis of their fit with the existing structure of the school (p. 24).

In human systems, differences generate tension, and the tension shifts as the system responds by self-organizing into new patterns that accommodate or reduce the tension. The new patterns emerge and are reinforced and amplified throughout the system. The phenomenon of emergence is how beliefs, attitudes, expectations, and cultural practices come into existence and continue to evolve as parts of the system interact to generate patterns in the greater whole. Although culture emerges without conscious planning or design by human beings, it can certainly be shaped to some degree when agents across the system make deliberate and informed choices about the patterns they want to generate at the whole, part, and the greater whole. This culture-generating process requires individuals and groups to deal with the inevitable tension that arises as the system responds to tension and moves toward coherence.

So What about Coherence and Culture?

In a complex adaptive system, as we explained above, system agents (individuals, ideas, beliefs, behaviors, practices, language, etc.)

interact so that they generate system-wide patterns. In this process of self-organization, emerging patterns influence the future interactions of the agents. Over time, subsequent interactions continue to influence the larger patterns, which evolve, influencing how agents think and act individually and collectively. We typically experience such emergent patterns that endure across time as "culture."

In human systems dynamics, we define **culture** as a set of emerging patterns that signal shared beliefs, values, and practices (including language, rituals, celebrations) that identify what it is to live, work, and play in the context of a specific system. Although anthropologists define culture as a system of beliefs and practices that emerge in a greater whole--say a community of people who share a common heritage, we are using the term to point to shared patterns at every scale of the system. Similarities across these cultural patterns (in classrooms, on campuses, in policy environments) enhance coherence across the whole, part, and the greater whole. The simple rule that is the focus of this chapter emphasizes that those of us who strive for generative changes in schools must keep these multiple scales in mind. We want to set conditions that build coherence up and down the system.

Think about the students in a 7th grade class. They interact in multiple ways through the day—playing, talking, arguing, and learning together. As they come to know each other early in the year, they establish patterns. Who sits together at lunch? Who is the class clown? Who answers all the hard questions? Those expectations set the patterns that characterize that particular class. Now, think about a new student entering the class. Or think about a student who doesn't conform to those expectations. The established patterns are usually so strong that the new student knows pretty quickly how to become a member of the class. And those patterns can be so strong that students who want to change their behaviors have a difficult time doing so. For example, when the whole class expects the class clown to make them laugh, almost anything that person does is seen as funny, causing a disruption that the person may not even intend. System-wide patterns of culture make it difficult for that student to move out of the clown role.

The same thing happens among the staff members and administrators, among students and parents—among the members of any school-based group as the patterns they generate contribute to the culture of the school. At the greater scale, the superintendent, administrative staff, board members, individual schools, and community members interact to generate the culture of the district. Figure 3.2 shows how subgroups may have their own patterns that ultimately generate the culture of the greater whole.

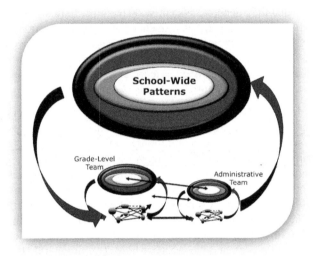

Figure 3.2: Model of multiple, scaled complex adaptive systems. This helps us visualize how interactions between and among the parts of a system can contribute to the greater whole.

If we have any hope of influencing a complex school system, we have to "attend to the whole, part, and greater whole" because that simple rule acknowledges the emergence of these cultural patterns up, down, and across the system.

When we limit our focus to one scale of the system, we limit our collective power. Often, we look at organizations like this and say they are working in "silos." The third grade teachers don't know what's happening in fifth grade. The cafeteria workers are not aware of how a shorter lunch schedule might influence the teachers' planning. The nurses don't think about the bus schedule. And the superintendent forgets what it was like to do playground duty each day. In such a fragmented system, we find little coherence and a limited capacity to adapt to the unpredictable future.

SO WHAT SHAPES EMERGENCE AND COHERENCE?

Emergence within and across these parts or layers of the system is a fact of life, whether or not we acknowledge it. Emergence itself is neither inherently good nor bad; it is neither "naughty nor nice." It just is. Sometimes what emerges seems productive and is welcomed—new friendships, new insights, and new plans. In general, these more desirable patterns are those that set conditions for necessary learning, adaptation, and coherence because those are the patterns that will help the system survive and thrive. Sometimes, however, emergence can lead to less welcome patterns. For example, anger is an emergent pattern that results from the interplay of tensions across the system. Bias and racism are also patterns emerging from tensions around difference, but they are not generative.

If we want to help encourage more generative patterns and move the system toward coherence, our only option is to try to influence the emerging patterns. We do that by noticing the patterns, by understanding what the patterns might mean for the system, and by setting conditions that influence or constrain the emerging patterns in appropriate ways. That means we need to understand how **constraints** work in a complex adaptive system.

Constraints Influence Emergence

Sometimes emergence happens quickly and in somewhat predictable ways. At other times, the process is gradual and completely surprising. The difference between these two paths depends on the constraints placed on the system's agents. When the agents have more freedom, they are not very constrained and their behaviors and interactions are more unpredictable. When constraint increases, the path and outcome of the emergent process will be more predictable. Because constraints in a complex system can never be complete and perfect, emergence is never absolutely predictable, but the predictability of self-organizing can be influenced by increasing or decreasing constraints on the system. Constraints limit randomness and increase certainty in a system. They shape the emerging patterns within, between, and among complex adaptive systems, so when we want to change the patterns at any scale of our system, we must take action that changes the constraints.

For example, classroom procedures are constraints that regulate or limit the multiple ways students might interact in the system.

- We constrain student conversation by framing questions and defining topics to keep students focused on the subject at hand.

- We use pre- and post-assessments to understand what students need to learn and constrain our instruction within that focus.

- We set expectations and classroom rules to constrain decisions about how students will interact with each other and their environment.

Sometimes classroom procedures over-constrain students' learning, forcing a level of compliance on them that actually limits creativity and engagement. On the other hand, we sometimes under-constrain learning with unclear expectations or unstructured time. That isn't particularly productive either. We have found that the Landscape Diagram helps us think about how varying levels of constraint help students at different points in their learning.

The Landscape Diagram, Constraints and Emergent Work

The Landscape Diagram is a graphic that helps people visualize the constraints in their systems (Eoyang and Holladay, 2004 http://www.hsdinstitute.org/about-hsd/what-is-hsd/faq-tools-and-patterns-of-hsd.html, adapted from Stacey, 2001). In the Landscape Diagram (Figure 3.3), two dimensions of the system are represented as a graph, with the X axis representing the degree of "certainty" in the system and the "Y" axis representing the degree of "agreement." We can use this diagram to think about specific issues in schools, like whether to require students to wear uniforms or how much instructional support a student might need. (You will notice that the Landscape Diagram is similar to the Learner's Landscape we discussed in Chapter 2.)

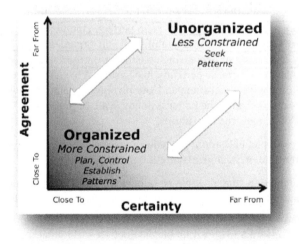

Figure 3.3: Landscape Diagram. This landscape is a two-dimensional representation of how increasing and decreasing constraints (more or less certainty and more or less agreement) can influence fit and functionality

The "certainty" axis refers to the predictability of the system. It provides a measure of how well individuals in the system can anticipate what is going to happen in the near future, along a spectrum from "close to" certainty (highly predictable) to "far from" certainty (little or no predictability). The "agreement" axis indicates the degree to which individuals in the system agree about what should happen in the system, from "close to agreement" to "far from agreement."

All activity in a system can be plotted on the Landscape Diagram along these two dimensions. There is not an absolutely "right" place on the landscape where the whole system should function, but various parts or processes within the system can most appropriately function in particular areas of the system, depending on the system's constraints.

Highly constrained conditions can be plotted in the lower left, where there is high agreement and high predictability. In a system or a part of a system that works efficiently, functions related to reliable, repeatable, concrete operations (more constrained) are depicted in the lower left corner of the graph because these functions require high levels of certainty and a high degree of agreement among the participants. For example, we would hope that people agree and are certain about payroll procedures, fire drills, bus schedules, and school calendars. These are issues that need to be highly constrained. On the Landscape Diagram, we label this area **Organized,** and the most effective way of functioning in the organized zone is detailed planning and control. The goal is to follow established patterns.

Far in the upper right, where there is little or no constraint, events are unpredictable, unknown, and random. Rather than following established patterns, this is where we must search for patterns. This area is labeled **Unorganized**. These are the surprising events of life—accidents, illnesses, and encounters with the unknown—that cannot be planned or accounted for in advance. We might also think of this zone as requiring creativity and exploration. Although this randomness is a necessary and sometimes welcome part of every human system, a classroom, campus, or school district cannot long survive if its patterns are exclusively in the unorganized zone. When we find ourselves in the unorganized zone, the best way to function is to stand in inquiry, seeking to see emergent patterns that increase the fitness of the system.

Events in the center are closer to agreement and certainty than in the unorganized zone, but are less constrained than in the organized zone. This is where the constraints support emergent or generative work (See Figure 3.4). In this zone, conditions are optimal for self-organization or transformation. Constraints allow for patterns to emerge as similarities, differences, and relationships that have meaning across space and time. To function here, agents strive to notice, understand, and influence patterns.

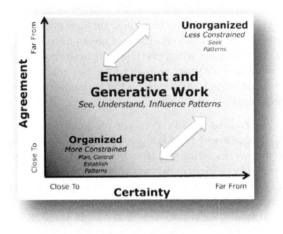

Figure 3.4: CAS Landscape Diagram implementation. This represents how more or less constraint in the system will support different kinds of work—organized, emergent, and unorganized.

Although a system operating in this zone experiences some constraint, a considerable degree of freedom allows for individual differences within patterns of coherence and similarity. This zone is where we can map activities such as interpersonal relationships, personal growth, and team development. In fact, most human activity happens in this zone, particularly when human beings are open to new information from inside and outside the system and when they are adapting in ways that sustain the work of the system. Although this adaptive, generative human activity involves some degree of coherence, it can neither be predicted nor controlled.

In schools, this emergent zone offers the optimal degree of constraint to support generative learning. When learning in classrooms functions primarily in this area of the Landscape Diagram, we see patterns of student engagement, problem-solving, connections between theory and practice, collaborative work, and critical analysis. It is here where inquiry-based approaches, like project-based learning and writing workshop are designed to optimize emergent learning. When teams of educators work in this area, we would expect them to be setting conditions for patterns of generative learning to emerge at multiple scales across the system.

In the upper right on the landscape, there is little constraint, which allows for greater freedom and exploration. As you increase constraints on an individual student or on the class, you shift on the landscape moving down and to the left. Creating classroom rules, limiting the field of study to a particular topic or lesson, asking for particular types of responses on assessments, selecting particular learning resources over others--these are all ways we constrain the learning environment and experiences to focus the patterns of student learning and growth.

The challenge is to find the amount and kinds of constraint that move the whole system toward coherence. The appropriate constraints may be different for the whole, the part, and the greater whole. Constraints that reduce tension at one point in a system may not work well enough at another point. Remember the two teachers who taught side by side, yet had very different expectations about their students' behaviors? In each classroom, constraints had emerged over time that allowed the teachers to believe they were doing their best job of helping students learn. But then when the two classes come together into a greater whole, the levels of constraint were not so clear and did not create coherence at that scale. The simple rule "Attend to patterns in the whole, the part, and the greater whole" is critical because in a system as large and complex as public education we have to consider how constraints set at one part of the system have an impact on other parts of the system. A national set of standards might seem perfectly reasonable at the federal level, but the high stakes testing that assess the attainment of those standards is over-constraining at the classroom level if those tests are seen as the only measures of learning.

Bureaucratic Action to Influence Constraints

At the campus level, we regulate or constrain the system by setting schedules for lunch, bell times for class periods, and expectations for how people move from one part of the building to another. Setting such constraints provides order and efficiency as we try to serve large numbers of students in one confined space. Shortened class periods might over-constrain the system because they limit the types of learning experiences for students. On the other hand, a fifteen-minute transition time between classes might under-constrain the system because that schedule would increase the unsupervised, self-directed time for students.

Across the district, standardized assessments, common curricular frameworks, and union contracts serve to constrain choices about what is taught when, how students are engaged, and how adults agree to work together.

At the national level, regulations constrain how federal funds are disseminated and how districts are held accountable for student learning.

In each of these instances, agents at some level of the system generate the constraints. At various scales, the system self-organizes toward greater coherence and reduced tension within those constraints. We reduce tension by focusing on teaching to the standards and spending significant time teaching students how to take standardized assessments. We reduce tension by engaging staff in developing the mandated scope and sequence of instruction. We reduce tension as we help students know and understand the rules for keeping a school building safe. Constraints at any one scale have an impact on the degrees of freedom at other scales.

When we set constraints at one scale, we have to attend to the whole, the part, and the greater whole to consider possible consequences for action. As we have tried to show, in the current reform climate across the US, setting high stakes around national standards may appear to be the most efficient way to know how well students are learning. People of good faith looked at student performance data from across the country and across past decades and recognized that some students experienced higher expectations and richer learning opportunities than others. They came to believe that shared, common expectations would help to build a stronger, more coherent and skilled citizenry as students left school and entered higher education or the workforce.

At the same time, none of us can lose sight of what happens in individual districts, schools, and classrooms as a result of those federal constraints on local instructional actions. Because education is a complex system--diverse, open, and nonlinear--we cannot assume that just because an answer makes sense at one scale it is going to automatically make sense at other scales of this national system. Nor can we assume that what works in one classroom is automatically going to be effective in any other classroom--or that it should drive what happens nationally. This understanding of constraint as bureaucratic action calls for educators at all levels to be clear about how to establish expectations that allow for local decisions that move toward systemic change at all scales.

Generative Teaching/Learning to Influence Constraints

Generative teaching/learning is about shifting the patterns of constraint that govern agents' actions to set conditions for patterns of learning that are most productive in the part, the whole, and the greater whole. Constraints, like emergence, are neither naughty nor nice. What gives them the appearance of being either naughty or nice is the degree to which those constraints actually help the system self-organize toward greater fitness, coherence, and sustainability. In Chapter 2, we argued for generative teaching/learning because it sets appropriate constraints on the system—so that the system can move toward fitness or coherence.

The question that should guide the work of school reformers is not, "How do we raise annual test scores?" but rather, "How can we set conditions to help this particular system function more generatively?" The question should not be, "How can we ensure that teachers implement particular programs with fidelity?" Instead, we should ask, "How can we unleash local creative insights and build adaptive capacity to address the challenges to learning in this district?" Understanding that we work in a complex system to influence local patterns toward generative teaching and learning, we come to recognize that the only way we can move toward this complex adaptive transformative stance is to stand in inquiry together, to use tools like Adaptive Action and the Landscape Diagram to see, understand, and generate options for action. Seeing patterns, understanding constraints on those patterns, and taking action to encourage emergence at the whole, the part, and the greater whole—this is the essence of adaptive capacity, which lies at the heart of transforming schools.

SO WHAT ABOUT ENSURING SUSTAINABILITY?

Sustaining positive change is a major challenge for school reformers. One way to move toward sustainability is to build adaptive capacity in the system. Adaptive capacity is the ability to see, understand, and influence patterns in response to the changes, challenges, and needs within and outside the system. Individuals respond to one another; groups interact to create stronger, more productive relationships; organizations develop policies and procedures that support adaptive and responsive action. When we think of system-wide adaptive capacity, this is what we see. Fullan calls it "collective capacity" (2010).

Adaptive capacity is the absolute commitment at all scales of the system to being sensitive and responsive in the near and far horizons, while remaining conscious of the inherent and unique constraints of any particular situation. Although there are generative options for action "close to home," people may make slightly different (and more generative) decisions if, at every point in their work, they think about potential constraints and emergent patterns at the whole, in the parts of that whole, and in the greater system. That means that classroom teachers should make decisions that build coherence across what individual students need, what works for the whole class, and what is consistent with campus goals and expectations. It means that principals need to think about individual students and families as well as teachers and stakeholders in the community. The goal is not absolute similarity or standardization, but continuing attempts to move toward coherence or fitness—an appropriate balance of similarity and difference across these scales.

If enough people in the system are working toward coherence across scales, the system is more likely to adapt appropriately to changing conditions. Coherent, emerging patterns at all scales are more likely to ensure the sustainability of a system's work over time, even when charismatic leaders move on and when once-abundant resources become scarce.

NOW WHAT? ENHANCE ADAPTIVE CAPACITY THROUGHOUT THE SYSTEM

Systems move toward coherence when people influence patterns at the part, whole, and greater whole as they respond to day-to-day challenges. As educators, when we understand how patterns emerge, we are better able to take wise action to assure alignment between and among agents and systems at each scale. When we take action to help the system move toward coherent patterns, we engage in generative learning from the classroom to the central office to the boardroom to the community. Here is what one teacher said to us about emergence and this simple rule:

> *So if I could talk to any new folks in the district, I would help people remember that transformation starts with you and the tiniest little degree of shift. If I move one degree here, the amount that trajectory over the long term is huge. It may not be a big shift here, but if you extend that out to the whole system, it's . . . well, it's an infinite trajectory. I guess that's what emergence is about.*

> *–High School Teacher*

We agree. Emergence is about infinite trajectories at every scale—the whole, the part, and the greater whole.

NOW WHAT? USE THESE RESOURCES TO LEARN MORE

Burns, D. (2007). *Systemic action research: a strategy for whole system change.* Bristol, UK: Policy Press.

Carse, James P. (1986). *Finite and infinite games.* New York: Ballantine Books.

Eoyang, G. H. (2012). Sir Issac's dog: learning for adaptive capacity. *The F. M. Duffy Reports, 17 (2),* 1-12.

Fullan, M. (2010). *All systems go: The change imperative for whole system reform.* Thousand Oaks, CA: Corwin Press and Ontario Principals' Council.

Hargreaves, A. & Fink (2006). *Sustainable leadership.* San Francisco: Jossey-Bass.

Holland, J (1998). *Emergence: From chaos to order.* Cambridge: Perseus Books.

Lee, V. E. & Ready, D. D (2007). *Schools within schools: possibilities and pitfalls of high school reform.* New York: Teachers College Press.

Levy, P. (1997). *Collective intelligence: mankind's emerging world in cyberspace.* New York: Plenum Trade.

Pappano, L. (2010). *Inside school turnarounds: ugent hopes, unfolding stories.* Cambridge, MA: Harvard Education Press.

CHAPTER 4:
Patterns

Simple Rule: See, understand, and influence patterns.

Once we understand how patterns emerge in complex adaptive systems, we can focus more specifically on the patterns we want to see in our systems and on the actions we can take to enhance those patterns. This helps us focus on what really matters in schools so that we can avoid the fragmentation that characterizes most bureaucracies. This chapter explains the significance of recurrent patterns in complex adaptive systems.

Central Challenge	To maintain focus
Simple Rule	See, understand, and influence patterns.
Concepts, Methods, and Models	• Patterns • Fractals • Conditions of CAS (Container, Difference, Exchange) • Simple Rules • Adaptive Action
Guiding Questions	• What are patterns in complex adaptive systems? • What are the conditions for self-organizing systems? • So how do we maintain focus on the patterns we want? • Now what? Shape patterns for adaptive capacity. • Now what? Use these resources to learn more.

Think about your last experience leading a group of learners—adults, youth, or children. These people may have known each other for some time. They came together to learn something new. Some came involuntarily; others came eagerly. They probably had at least some common understanding of the purpose of their coming together, but each one began with different expectations about what they would learn and how they could contribute. They each brought different background knowledge about the topic. Once they came together, how did they begin to engage in the work? How did they explore the topic with others? How did they express their own learning? You probably cannot answer these questions about each student, but by the end of the session, you could be sure that they left the session with some common understandings.

How does that happen? The answer is self-organization, a process through which individuals act in interdependent ways to generate system-wide patterns. As we explained in Chapter 2, generative teaching/learning is essentially an adaptive and self-organizing process that happens in human complex adaptive systems. Individuals constantly self-organize as they interact with people, events, opportunities, and challenges around them, and new patterns emerge. Individuals (and groups) can take action that sometimes appears to make self-organization work better—patterns emerge faster or more powerfully, people are more effectively engaged, and tasks get accomplished smoothly. On the other hand, sometimes they feel at the mercy of environmental influences that prevent effective or efficient work. What makes the difference in what patterns emerge and how they shape the future behavior of the system?

In this chapter we explore the third simple rule:

See, understand, and influence patterns.

This chapter explains how patterns form in complex adaptive human systems and how we individually or collectively influence the patterns that shape our lives. Once we understand that we influence those patterns, we can begin to understand how to move the patterns toward coherence. At that point, we are building the adaptive capacity of our system.

WHAT ARE PATTERNS IN COMPLEX ADAPTIVE SYSTEMS?

As we explained in earlier chapters, when we talk about system **patterns**, we mean the **similarities, differences, and connections that have meaning across space and time.** In more familiar terms, we mean that patterns are the multiple ways we come to see and understand our worlds around us. All of learning—the baby's earliest recognition of mama's voice, scent, and feel, a child's learning to read, a young adult's learning about raising children—we seek to understand our worlds by building categories of how things are similar, how they are different, and how one thing is or can be connected to others. We make meaning of our lives by understanding the patterns we see (and feel, smell, and hear). And we bring order to our lives by noticing patterns out of the multiple random events, actions, and interruptions in our day-to-day existence.

Patterns form spontaneously and perpetually in complex adaptive human systems. Think about our earlier explanation of human systems dynamics: Agents in human systems (people, thoughts, bodies, ideas, concepts, groups, etc.) interact, forming system-wide patterns. They come together in groups that are similar. They may seek those who are like them or avoid those who are different. Human beings connect with other human beings; they engage with ideas, bring random thoughts together to create new perspectives. Ideas come together in logical, useful ways to create new concepts. The patterns that are the most resilient resonate across the system and eventually come to characterize the culture of the system.

Those dominant patterns, in turn, influence subsequent behavior within the system. How any person or group behaves is influenced by the cultural and societal patterns they grew up in. How people see and interpret their worlds depends on their perspectives or worldviews. Societies codify the patterns they desire by establishing rules and regulations that inform everyone's behavior.

"Learning" in a complex adaptive system is the process of coming to see and understand the patterns that make up our lives. **"Change" involves envisioning and establishing patterns that are more fit or sustainable than the ones we currently observe.** As we have pointed out, we refer to the potential for creating more appropriate patterns as **adaptive capacity**. Developing adaptive capacity for individuals and institutions is the role of the leader and the teacher.

As we discussed in Chapter 3, we see similar patterns at multiple scales of complex adaptive systems (CASs). Children often mimic the patterns of their parents. Political patterns of partisanship or collaboration are reflected in (or are reflective of) the ways local teams or communities work together in varying degrees of cooperation and compassion. Bosses and leaders are instructed to "walk their talk" because their behavior is a model for others. Fashion and music made popular in movies and other media are emulated by individuals. The patterns at one scale influence the behavior of the system at other scales, and as a system becomes more coherent, the self-similarity of those patterns at the various scales increases.

This tendency for patterns to be similar at varying scales of a system is characteristic of **fractals.** In mathematics, a fractal is a geometric figure, where patterns of the parts are similar to the patterns of the whole. The pictures in Figure 4.1 are examples of fractal structures, one from nature and the other generated by a computer.

Figure 4.1: Images of fractals. In these two pictures of fractal

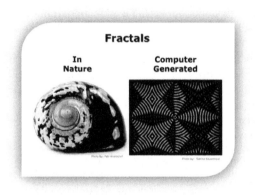

structures, notice how the parts at the smaller scales look like the parts that are larger. The same shapes (patterns) are repeated across the shape of the whole.

In mathematics, a fractal is formed from a particular kind of equation when every answer feeds back into the process to create the next answer. As this nonlinear process is repeated from different starting points, a pattern is created that is self-similar across scale. A similar process works in biological systems, when DNA influences highly interdependent, repetitive processes to generate coherent patterns in living structures. We experience teaching and learning as a similar process: An experience results from past patterns and influences patterns of the future, over time, coherent patterns emerge for individuals, groups, and institutions. Three things influence the resulting fractal pattern: 1) the starting point; 2) the basic instruction; 3) the repetition or iteration of the process.

In this book we are suggesting that the seven simple and radical rules are the "instructions" that will generate fractals of generative teaching/learning across a school system by providing the basic instruction that is repeated across multiple interactions.

So here's what we know about how patterns work in generative teaching/learning:

- Patterns are how we make sense of our experiences.
- Patterns consist of similarities, differences and connections within the system.
- Fractals often show up at different places across the system.
- Although we can't control complex systems, we can take adaptive actions to strengthen some patterns and diminish others.

Noticing, naming, and describing patterns, however, does not help us influence our systems. The real power of looking at a system through the lens of human systems dynamics is that it helps us to understand the underlying dynamics—how patterns are shaped and how they evolve through the process of self-organization. When we understand how patterns form, we can be more intentional and sensitive as we set conditions to shape them.

WHAT ARE THE CONDITIONS FOR SELF-ORGANIZING SYSTEMS?

Patterns in human systems are not static. They evolve in response to changing conditions. Sometimes the evolution is slow and gradual; sometimes it is abrupt and dramatic. When we notice these changing patterns in complex systems, we are watching the process of self-organization. If we want to influence complex systems (like learning) we need to understand what shapes those changes. What are the conditions that influence, constrain, and inform those emerging patterns?

In her early research, Glenda proposes three conditions that influence the speed, path, and direction of self-organizing patterns (Eoyang, 2002). Further, she says that individuals can learn to see, understand, and influence those conditions to shift patterns toward increased productivity and improved relationships. She names these conditions **containers, differences, and exchanges** (C,D,E).

HSD practitioners analyze what is happening in terms of these three conditions. Figure 4.2 suggests central questions that can guide such an analysis. When they are able to recognize a pattern in terms of the conditions—containers, differences, and exchanges—that constrain the agents, then they can take intentional action to shift one or more of the conditions and, thereby, influence patterns as they emerge. The paragraphs following Figure 4.2 further explain container, difference, and exchange in human systems.

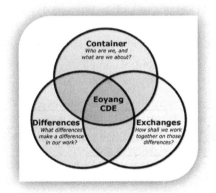

Figure 4.2: Conditions for Self-Organizing. Glenda Eoyang identified three conditions that influence the speed, path, and direction of self-organization in complex adaptive systems.

Containers: Who Are We, and What Are We About?

First, emergent patterns require **containers** to bound the system—to hold it together so that agents can interact in such a way that they can form patterns. Containers may be physical—like offices, houses, city limits. In schools, particular locations like the library, the cafeteria, and the nurse's office may also serve as containers. Containers may also be conceptual, like powerful ideas, cultural identity, or loyalty to a charismatic leader. For example, in schools, we often see a district or campus self-organize in response to a popular initiative or a well-loved leader. Or groups of people (communities? cliques? gangs?) can self-organize around a shared cultural belief or practice.

Containers organize people. Teams, departments, classes, faculties are all examples of ways people organize in schools to accomplish one or more tasks. These people containers are sometimes about a shared **task**, but they may also be about a shared **identity**—people with shared characteristics—or about **affiliation**—people who enjoy being together. If all three of these functions (task, identity, and affiliation) are at work, the container is particularly strong and is likely to hold over time. For example, if a group of innovative writing teachers (identity) who enjoy being together (affiliation) decide to establish an after-school writing club at their local middle school (task), we are seeing a strong container at work.

Time can also be a container---this month's plan, today's work, six-week grading period, fifth-grade year, high school years. We bound time by the expectations and events that are held within.

Containers can also organize concepts or ideas. Think about the Ten Commandments, the *Declaration of Independence*, and rock music. Whether a single document, a category or a genre, these conceptual containers function to hold systems of thought and action together over time. Sometimes a container refers to a cultural group (the Ten Commandments), and sometimes it simply points to an amorphous cluster of similar ideas or preferences, (rock music). In schools, we can point to documents or artifacts that organize concepts, like textbooks, syllabi, standards, curriculum guides, and tests. We can also point to movements or trends in education as conceptual containers, like Progressivism, Whole Language, and the recent accountability movement.

Sometimes containers are nested (classrooms; campuses; districts; states; and the federal system). Sometimes containers overlap (a group of students may belong to the same soccer team, the same grade level, and the gaming club that meets after school). Our multiple identities often delineate overlapping container boundaries. Gender, ethnicity, race, sexual orientation, socio-economic status may work in this way because they are always present, and in some places they can become containers that make a difference in the dynamics of a system.

Containers are essentially a way for us to notice and name similarities—similarities across time, space, people, and concepts. And systems must have at least some degree of similarity for the individual agents (whether people or ideas) to "hang together" long enough for system-wide patterns to emerge. Those system-wide patterns may then reinforce and sustain the container. And the system goes on.

When focusing on powerful human system containers, HSD practitioners ask themselves, "Who are we and what are we about?" The answer to that question points to the relevant containers in our work. In this book, we consider generative teaching/learning as the overarching container in our work. This question would point to the multiple containers that would be relevant to supporting and sustaining generative teaching/learning in schools.

We believe that inappropriate container management is one reason school reform has not sustained. Reform efforts frequently focus too much on superficial or temporary containers--the latest technology mandate, the most recent reading program, textbook adoptions, new grading systems. It is easy to invest time and energy into the reform effort of the month or the persuasive leader rather than on the variable and complex containers that support and enhance student learning. Over time, an initiative focused on a temporary container will lose its appeal; the charismatic leader will move on; or the project will run out of money. Without the focal container to hold the system together, the reform effort can lose its identity or its reason for being. In that case, it cannot sustain.

Time Out for Reflection
In one challenge you face, what containers serve to hold the whole thing together? What containers seem to divide people? How have ideas become containers? Space? Time? Interests? Identity?

Difference: What Differences Make a Difference to Our Work?

It's not enough for a system to have similarities that function to contain the system. Another essential condition is **difference**. Although people share similarities, each individual is unique; different from all others in innumerable ways. That is also true of conceptual containers. Although an ideological container (like the current accountability movement in U.S. schools) may have many widely held assumptions and expectations, we also see differences in perspective, in focus, and in policy recommendations. In human systems, just as in healthy ecological systems, diversity is essential.

Any one container will have too many differences to count or consider all of them, but some differences matter more than others. These "differences that make a difference" become the target issues or goals or subjects of the work in that container. In a way, these differences or diversity across a system give the system life. They hold the potential energy of the system and fuel thought and action that would otherwise be monotonous or static. We might say that a system with few differences that matter is "stuck in a rut" and that its agents would be in danger of ceasing to work as a system—the system-wide pattern that emerges in a complex adaptive system must have difference. Without difference in contrast to the similarity, there is no pattern, and, therefore, no system.

Difference may show up in at least two ways. The first is "difference in kind" between specific characteristics of the agents in the system, such as differences between math knowledge and interpersonal skills. The second way difference shows up is "difference or variability in degree" along a continuum for one specific characteristic, such as one person increasing his or her math knowledge over time.

In schools, the first kind of difference is central to the business of schooling—to focus on different measures of student achievement. But in many schools, we focus only on differences in achievement without paying attention to other potentially critical differences–differences in gender, ethnicity, socio-economic status, family stability, for example. If we focus only on differences in test scores, we ignore many of the differences that might make the system-wide patterns engaging, effective, or interesting. If an institution focuses on a only few differences, especially if those differences are not relevant or engaging to stakeholders, the institution itself loses its vitality as people disengage. Individuals and groups soon drop out—metaphorically and literally. Our challenge in human systems dynamics is to focus on the "differences that make a difference." In schools, we are particularly interested in the differences relevant to system-wide patterns such as generative learning and effective teaching.

The second way that difference shows up in a system has to do with the difference in degree, rather than difference in kind. These differences are also clearly relevant to our work in schools. The mission of schooling, after all, is to "move" individuals from knowing less to knowing more about particular concepts or skills. We all agree about that. The controversies come when we try to decide what combination of concepts and skills is most significant and what levels of performance are acceptable. Controversies also arise when we try to determine where students begin on those continua and how far they can and should move in a given time frame.

The questions educators should ask themselves if they are interested in generative teaching/learning are "What differences make a difference in this system?" and "What does that mean for the focus of our work?" Our challenge in HSD is to focus on the differences that influence the emergence of generative learning throughout the system.

Exchange: How Shall We Work Together on Those Differences?

The third condition is **exchange**—how information and other resources are shared and disseminated across the system. Sometimes these exchanges are transactions among agents. People talk and listen, give and take, conduct individual and collaborative inquiry, and act and observe one other. They share their stories, request help, analyze data, report findings, create artwork, publish curricula, and sometimes dance and play together. All these exchanges (and many more) support self-organization or the emergence of system-wide patterns.

In schools where generative teaching/learning is the pattern we seek, our challenge is to support and amplify the exchanges that might potentially support and sustain that pattern. Do our exchanges include the voices of all participants? Do they open possibilities for new information and new perspectives? Do they focus on differences that make a difference for generative learning? Do they acknowledge multiple overlapping and nested containers that are relevant to our work? In Chapter 5, we address those powerful, generative exchanges in much greater detail.

After considering our options, we might organize "communities of practice" as a new container where teachers might engage in transformative exchanges about their concerns—differences they have decided might make a difference to their students. Or we might decide that a weekly e-mail to students' families and interested community members could increase the community members' common understandings and perspectives about targeted goals. These are just a few examples; the actions that might influence generative exchanges are unlimited.

> **Time Out for Reflection**
> *Think of a challenge you are facing with colleagues or students. How might you shift your exchanges? More exchanges? Fewer? Longer feedback loops? Longer or shorter messages? Face-to-face or online? How might those shifts influence the patterns?*

Conditions Working Together toward Self-Organization

Each condition—container, difference, and exchange—influences self-organization by constraining the dynamics of the system in particular ways. Small or few containers speed up self-organization by increasing constraint. More containers or larger containers will slow the process down as constraints decrease. More differences in a system introduce confusion, slowing down efforts at self-organization, while large differences give greater latitude for change. Tightly coupled systems with many exchanges self-organize more quickly than systems with fewer exchanges or where the members of the system are less connected.

Highly Constrained		Highly Unconstrained
Small, tight, closed containers	**Containers**	Large, loose, leaky containers
Few, small differences	**Differences**	Many, large differences
Short, tightly coupled exchanges	**Exchanges**	Long, loosely coupled exchanges

Figure 4.3: Continuum of constraint and the three conditions for self-organization. The three conditions function as constraints on the process of self-organizing, or emergence.

Figure 4.3 suggests how shifts in these three conditions can constrain the self-organizing dynamics (the emergence) in a system. More constraint leads to more similarity; less constraint opens the system to more variability. Clearly, this explains more about how constraints work in the Landscape Diagram we introduced in Chapter 3. More constraint moves the system toward the control and uniformity in the lower left corner of the Landscape Diagram (see Figures 3.3 and 3.4). Less constraint moves the system toward the upper right, more random area of the Landscape Diagram. The underlying conditions of this emerging landscape/system (container, difference, and exchange) hold the potential for constraining the system in different ways and, therefore for influencing the path of self-organization.

Classroom instruction can provide concrete examples of how these conditions and system constraints work. No matter what the grade level or the content area, when students are first learning a complex concept, they need more constraint (guidance and support), and as they become more knowledgeable and proficient, they can function with less constraint (more independence and more opportunity to explore). Many teachers call this the "gradual release model" (Pearson and Gallagher, 1983).

Leslie and her colleagues write about how teachers made complex choices about how to shape the constraints in their high school English classrooms (Patterson, Wickstrom, Roberts, Araujo, & Hoki, 2010). For example, Jennifer, a high school English teacher, faced the considerable challenge of helping twelfth-grade English learners deal with British literature. Jennifer said that she used whole-group discussions (container) to focus on a narrow range of issues (differences) and helped students think and talk (exchanges) as they connected familiar topics to unfamiliar British literature. She said, "I use classroom discussions as anticipatory sets—I get them talking and thinking about something in their own lives and then I move into, 'Well, let's see what Hamlet thinks about that . . .'"

In her letter to the research team at the end of the year, Jennifer explained her approach to *Beowulf* and other challenging literary selections:

> *With this unit, I wanted to focus on the idea of "culture" and try to find parallels between cultures, even cultures far removed from modern day. Before reading this piece, I asked students to answer six questions about their cultures—places, objects, values or beliefs, and rituals that were important to their community or culture, as well as identify one "monster" feared by their community or culture. I gave the students information about the culture of the Anglo-Saxons before starting. About halfway through the story of* Beowulf, *we stopped and answered these six questions again, but this time about the Anglo-Saxons. It seemed to be an effective way to help them think about how history and life conditions affect the values a culture adopts.*

After this unit, students then wrote definition essays, using the questions about their own community to guide their topic choices. Students read definition essays from professional writers for examples, and then students chose an artifact, a term, an event, or ritual to define in their essay.

This example also illustrates how Jennifer began with more constraints in the system—focusing the students on the six questions. Once she provided students with a learning scaffold, example, or specific task and ensured that students could use it successfully, she then allowed more student autonomy as she invited them to choose a topic for their essay. At first she set conditions with a fairly small and familiar container or focus, asking the students to consider their personal experiences, which narrowed the range of differences each student was asked to consider. She began with non-threatening exchanges—in whole group discussions, and then gradually moved to more independent and open-ended exchanges as each student composed an entire essay.

Every thoughtful teacher can name how this stepping-in-and-backing-off process works with particular students, in specific content areas. When they do this, teachers are, in fact, increasing and decreasing constraints in the system. The underlying dynamic has to do with the teacher's power (and responsibility) to set the three conditions (CDE) that make for the appropriate level of constraint in the system—the appropriate level of support—so that students can take reasonable learning risks and move toward their learning goals.

We could say that, when teachers set appropriate constraints, they are enabling students to work and learn within their zones of proximal development, or ZPD (Vygotsky, 1978).

All three conditions—container, difference, and exchange—are essential. If, as agents in the system, we want to influence the system's path, we can take action that amplifies, damps, or shifts one or more of these conditions. When we tweak one of the conditions, the others will shift in response. They are integrally related and interdependent. This means that we do not have to introduce complicated or long-term, whole-system restructuring to make significant changes. Small actions can trigger significant movement across the system—when we know enough about the relevant containers, differences and exchanges and when we choose our actions wisely.

Table 4.1 suggests how educators might do a "CDE Analysis" of a particular challenge in their work, which we might call a "sticky issue." Sticky issues are nagging problems that we just can't seem to solve. They are typically so big or so complex that it is hard to know where to begin. Adaptive Action, of course, is what we would advise, and this CDE Analysis helps us answer the questions "What?" and "So What?" What are the conditions (containers, differences, and exchanges) that are relevant to this issue? What patterns do those CDEs form? Are those desirable patterns or not? Do they seem to be generative or adaptive? Do they feel coherent with other patterns? Once we have done this analysis, we can search for options for action that will most likely shift the containers, differences, and exchanges—in other words, options for action that will shift the conditions for this self-organizing system and which, therefore, will influence the patterns. Obviously, we want to strengthen or expand the generative and coherent patterns, and we want to damp or marginalize the undesirable patterns. The next section suggests how to think about these options for action.

Table 4.1: CDE Analysis Sheet. Educators can use this sheet to describe and analyze their sticky issues.

Sticky Issue:				
Containers	Differences	Exchanges	Pattern	Generative? Coherent?

SO HOW DO WE MAINTAIN FOCUS ON THE PATTERNS WE WANT?

Individuals who have adaptive capacity have what they need to set conditions for generative teaching/learning. They can see the patterns in their world; they understand how those patterns are shaping their experiences; and they take informed action to change or sustain those patterns. In fact, people do this intuitively across their lives as they learn to walk and talk, to engage with others in socially acceptable ways, and to make their places in the world. Two core strategies emerge from HSD that help individuals and groups engage in generative learning in shared and intentional ways, leveraging the power of their understanding to deal with the uncertainty they encounter. First, **simple rules** establish a context of shared expectations and coherence across the system. Then **Adaptive Action** provides a map for iterative reflection and learning that moves the system forward.

Simple Rules Provide Focus

As we discussed in Chapter 1, we can use simple rules to set the conditions to generate the patterns we want. Based on our work in schools, we propose a set of simple—yet radical—rules to influence the containers,

differences, and exchanges at all scales in a system, generating the
conditions that have great likelihood of shaping the patterns of generative
teaching/learning. Table 4.2 points out how these Simple Rules might
influence the conditions in a classroom or among faculty colleagues.

*Table 4.2. How simple rules for generative learning address Eoyang's three conditions of
self-organizing systems.*

Simple Rules for Generative Teaching/ Learning	Simple Rule: Focus on Containers, Differences or Exchanges
Teach and learn in every interaction.	Teaching and learning are exchanges that focus on significant differences.
Pay attention to the whole, the part, and the greater whole.	This rule helps us notice the exchanges between and among nested and overlapping containers in the system.
See, understand, and influence patterns.	Patterns emerge in containers, and this rule leads to exchanges through which we work on those patterns.
Recognize and build on assets of self and others.	This rule requires exchanges focusing on assets, which are one way we can think of individual and group differences.
Seek the true and the useful.	"Seeking" points to potential exchanges about true and useful differences (the ones that make a difference to the system).
Be curious; embrace uncertainty; act with courage.	This rule recommends how we approach our exchanges within particular containers, about relevant differences.
Engage in joyful practice.	Engagement is an exchange; practice is about focusing on particular differences in relevant containers.

Time Out for Reflection

*Focus on how <u>one</u> of the seven simple rules for
generative teaching/learning might play out in your
work. If everyone in that situation followed this one
Simple Rule, how might the containers, differences, and
exchanges be more or less constrained? How might the
overall patterns in the system change?*

Adaptive Action Provides Focus

Paulo Freire wrote that people are not objects, but subjects of history (Freire, 1970). In other words, humans don't have to be victimized by the patterns around them. They can influence those patterns and become actors in the stories unfolding in their own communities. Many people refer to such a creative capacity as "agency." In human systems dynamics, we call it "adaptive capacity," and our goal is to support the development of adaptive capacity of individuals and groups. HSD methods and models can help people build the capacity to see the patterns around them, understand the implications, constraints, and conditions of those patterns, and take wise action to shift those patterns. The question remains: How can educators use this knowledge of patterns and the underlying conditions to transform their systems and generate patterns for radical change?

In Chapter 2, we suggested **Adaptive Action** as a way to frame a reflective inquiry process. Although human systems may seem hopelessly complex and unpredictable, through Adaptive Action, we can explore the patterns that emerge from the dynamics of these systems and respond appropriately. In other words, people can learn from their experiences and work together to influence systems toward more coherence and greater sustainability.

Figure 4.4: Adaptive Action cycle. This recursive inquiry/action cycle drives generative teaching/learning.

NOW WHAT? SET CONDITIONS FOR ADAPTIVE CAPACITY

No single approach ensures generative learning in a classroom, school, or district. Students, teachers, situations are all unique, so no single magic answer creates generative learning at every place and in every exchange. There is no "best practice" for generative learning. What we offer, in place of best practice, are descriptions of patterns that we believe hold the potential to help build adaptability and responsiveness in school systems. Then, as school systems and the individuals that inhabit them become more adaptive and responsive, they will be able to meet individual needs, engaging students in developing their adaptive capacity as well.

We think that administrators and teachers should strive for "generative" patterns. As we have explained previously, those are the patterns that will sustain the system. Of course, there are no absolute "best patterns." The educators in each system should work together to decide what patterns they want to see and how to shift conditions toward those patterns, but we do have an example to consider.

Funded in 2007-10 by the National Writing Project, a research team in North Texas worked with twelve teachers across the state to document inquiry-based writing instruction for English learners. In part, their findings (based on teacher interviews, written reflections, and classroom observations) documented five patterns of instruction in these classrooms of responsive and highly effective teachers (Wickstrom, Patterson, and Araujo, 2011). We see these five patterns as consistent with the kind of adaptive learning that we value in schools. Most readers will notice that these patterns resonate with other research-based approaches advocated for all students:

- **Empathy and Responsiveness** – Where teachers and learners are aware of and responsive to each others' needs and strengths in the learning setting.

- **Meaning Making** – Teachers and learners seek to see, understand, and influence patterns in texts, in relationships, and in individual performance.

- **Inquiry** – Each person in the learning situation stands in inquiry, seeking to understand his or her own and others' learning needs at any point in time.

- **Authenticity** – Students are engaged in reading a wide range of texts and in considering issues that are authentic for them and relevant to their lives.
- **Mediation for Learning** – Teachers find ways to help students connect ideas and to bridge past knowledge with current learning.

Human systems dynamics teaches us that if we clearly understand the patterns we want to see, we can take wise action to shift conditions to amplify these patterns where they exist; to damp patterns that are counter to these; and to identify new actions that help to generate the patterns we want. Because they are influenced by individual and group dynamics, steps can be taken at all scales to help set the conditions that support these patterns. Educators who seek sustainable and generative teaching and learning see, understand, and influence patterns in their systems.

NOW WHAT? USE THESE RESOURCES TO LEARN MORE

Ball, P. (2011). *Nature's patterns: A tapestry in three parts.* New York: Oxford University Press. (Reprint edition in 3 volumes: Shapes, Flow, and Branches, 2011, Oxford University Press).

Holladay, R. and Quade, K. (2008). *Influencing patterns for change: A primer for Human Systems Dynamics Professionals.* CreateSpace. Las Vegas.

NOVA. *Hunting the hidden dimension.* Produced and directed by Michael Schwarz and Bill Jersey. Aired August 24, 2011, on PBS.

Meadows, D. H. (2008). *Thinking in systems: A primer.* White River Junction, Vt.: Chelsea Green Publishers.

Schmoker, M. J. (2011). *Focus: Elevating the essentials to radically improve student learning.* Alexandria, VA: Association for the Supervision and Curriculum Development.

CHAPTER 5:
Assets

Simple Rule:
Recognize and build on assets of self and others.

No one works in isolation in a school system. From a human systems dynamics perspective, it is critical to work together, to focus on everyone's strengths, and to build collaborative relationships. That will help us build adaptive capacity in ourselves and in others throughout the system. This chapter explains how to build collaboration through generative engagements among students, teachers, and all the stakeholders in schools.

Central Challenge	To encourage collaboration
Simple Rule	Recognize and build on assets of self and others.
Concepts, Methods, and Models	• Generative Engagement • Patterns
Guiding Questions	• What are generative engagements? • So how do we set conditions for generative engagement? • So what about collaboration? • Now what? Leverage assets for adaptive capacity. • Now what? Use these resources to learn more.

When we build on assets in ourselves and others, we stand ready to work together toward shared goals, and we are better prepared to deal with the inevitable conflicts that happen in complex systems. Here's a comment from a school district staff member that suggests what can happen in a system that focuses on assets:

> *I think the biggest thing I've learned is just not to overreact, not to make assumptions about what somebody's asking or saying. Just last week, I got a phone call from the district office that said, "You need to be here in the morning. We need a conversation." I just said, "OK, see you in the morning." I didn't worry about it. In the past I probably would not have slept. So I didn't worry about it. I knew that I had done everything I could, and I was ready to have that conversation to figure out next steps.*

> *–Department Supervisor*

Typically, school reform initiatives attempt to fix the system by getting to the root cause of the troubles in a school district. It's like old medical models—find out what's ailing the patient and address that problem. Prescriptions, therapy, life support—even amputation and lobotomy—have been used as methods for dealing with symptoms. So it has been with public education. The traditional focus has been on what is wrong. This deficit perspective is captured in the following assumptions.

- Best practices, when implemented with rigor and fidelity, work in every place. If they are not working, it's somebody's fault.

- It's possible to measure the effectiveness of the whole system by testing individual performance on narrowly defined learning standards. When individuals don't perform, we know who is at fault.

- Schools and school districts that perform below standards will improve if they are given additional resources and subjected to stricter, more frequent regulatory performance checks. That is how we can find out who is at fault, and hold them accountable.

- It is most effective to take over or close schools and school districts that have not performed well over time. After all, it's their fault for failing.

We reject this deficit approach. In complex adaptive systems, it's much more powerful to build on what's already working to move toward a robust and sustainable system. With that in mind, we propose our fourth simple rule for the transformation of teaching and learning:

Recognize and build on assets of self and others.

In this chapter we explain how to set conditions for patterns that honor differences among people, that celebrate their contributions, and foster collaboration. This discussion is based on Generative Engagement, a model developed by Royce and her colleague, Mary Nations (http://patternsandpossibilities.squarespace.com/).

WHAT ARE GENERATIVE ENGAGEMENTS?

Generative Engagement is based on the assumption that each individual is a unique mix of physical, emotional, cognitive, and spiritual experiences and perspectives. Individuals come to school from different homes, bringing with them their distinct personalities, experiences, and cultural knowledge. Besides those individual differences, we are who (and where) we are because of historical, socio-economic, cultural, and political dynamics in larger systems. That means that our differences in power and status are also in the mix. Our expectations are filtered through perceptions of these power differences, as well as our partial knowledge of one another and our reliance on stereotypes. With all this potential for misunderstanding and conflict, how can people bring diverse experiences, beliefs, and dispositions together to generate new and shared perspectives? Generative Engagement offers a way to do that. The more specific challenge for educators is to work across these myriad differences toward productive learning outcomes, regardless of potential conflicts in any given moment. How can we collaborate as we move into generative sustainable relationships, in spite of the differences that divide us? How can we—as teachers and leaders in schools--find ways to build more responsive and generative relationships?

As leaders in schools and other organizations, both Royce and Mary saw a major barrier in the ways people built (or failed to build) working relationships across difference. They also saw that school reformers pointed to collaboration as a major challenge to successful school change. Clearly, collaboration requires people to work across their many differences. Most of the literature about inclusion and diversity spoke to differences in gender, race, ethnicity, language, sexual preference, and class, but Royce and Mary recognized that even more subtle differences—opinions, preferences, experiences—can also create conflict and misunderstanding in systems.

The problem is not only that people don't know how to accommodate the larger "isms" that divide groups. They just don't know how to negotiate effectively across significant differences, to collaborate toward shared goals. In human systems dynamics terms, they don't seem to know how to set conditions for the system to self-organize in collaborative ways. (See Chapter 4 for conditions for self-organizing systems.) Instead, people tend to create **containers** that connect them only to people with whom they identify, containers that isolate them from everyone else. They focus on **differences** that cannot be changed, rather than ones that can be negotiated. Their **exchanges** are exclusionary, biased, or even bigoted, as they connect with others in ways that reinforce similarities and discount or punish difference. A system's continued inability to accommodate difference and support collaboration contributes to a lack of coherence and endangers sustainability across the whole.

Mary and Royce believed that understanding the dynamics of these emergent patterns could help people think about shifting their patterns toward more effective and efficient (generative) collaboration. Using the CDE model, they considered the conditions for self-organization that might trigger the emergence of responsive and generative relationships, and derived what they call the **Generative Engagement** model (Figure 5.1).

An amazing teacher tells a story that serves to illustrate the tension that can build in these differences—and how that tension can sometimes be released in generative ways:

> *We were reading an Eve Bunting story called Flyaway Home. The kid in the book is homeless, and he feels "vulnerable," and we were talking about what it means to be "vulnerable." I have one student who's famous for going "I don't know" whenever I ask him questions. We were talking about what "I don't know" means. I said that I think it means, "You're afraid to say something so you put up this shield of 'I don't know.' Instead of telling me what you don't know, tell me what you do know." And he says, "There is something I do know." I said, "What do you know?" And he says, "I feel vulnerable." And that absolutely broke the tension, the conflict that I felt with him. Because then it became a matter of, "Well, let's talk about how that feels. I've felt that way, too. What does that mean? What do you feel vulnerable about?"*

> *–Fifth-grade teacher*

This is **generative engagement**—an exchange among people with equal power, sincerely standing in inquiry about what the other feels and thinks, ready to move forward together. Once this student and teacher stepped into this generative space, they were able to work collaboratively to understand this children's story and connect it to their lives.

SO HOW DO WE SET CONDITIONS FOR GENERATIVE ENGAGEMENT?

When we are involved in relationships that focus on deficits, we see and feel patterns that are stressful or hurtful. We might consider the patterns around us and ask, "What patterns would be more useful or beneficial to the system?" We might want to shift conditions in the system to create patterns of interaction that encourage people to work together, across their differences, to build system resilience and sustainability at all scales. Those patterns would help the system move toward fitness and coherence, both internally and externally. Three of those generative patterns that we want to create and sustain are **reciprocity, authenticity, and justice**.

Generative engagements require that people contribute what they can as they build on each other's strengths. We call that larger pattern **reciprocity**. Generative engagements let people know they are respected and honored for their unique contributions and challenges. We call that pattern **authenticity**. Finally, generative engagements ensure that the needs and abilities of individuals and groups are considered in the context of the whole. We call that pattern **justice**.

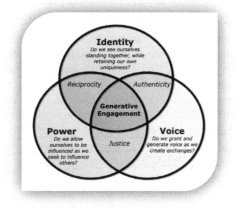

Figure 5.1: The Generative Engagement Model. We use the CDE configuration to show conditions that can enable individuals and groups to negotiate across their differences to work together collaboratively.

We use the CDE model to name conditions we believe will generate these patterns. In Figure 5.1 the top circle, **Identity**, names the container that binds us together. **Power** names the difference that matters in any generative relationship. **Exchanges** in generative engagements

Who Are We? Shared Identity

The first question, "Who are we?" is about our identity. Identity is how we name our shared similarity as we stand together in a given relationship. We may have shared values and beliefs that make it easy to stand together. On the other hand we may have vastly different values and beliefs. If we are to create generative engagements, however, we have to find some common ground where we stand together. Who are we as fellow learners in this classroom? Who are we together on this campus? What is our relationship to one another as we work together to build a functional, productive school system? This question calls us to a shared identity—a sharing of who we are together and how we can work together toward shared goals.

Shared identity does not ask us to ignore our own identity or personality. We can retain our individuality in our relationships, as we stand in shared space to take on a task together. We identify together around ideas and principles; we share geographical location; or we care about shared affinities. To be in a productive relationship requires that we share significant issues like direction and goals. The more strongly we share a common identity, the stronger our relationship will be.

In a classroom, teacher and students come together in a shared relationship of teaching and learning that focuses them on the common goals of the class or course. Each has unique perspectives, needs, and assets, and in generative engagements, they come together in mutual support. The same is true of the different roles taken on at the building level or district office or among the board of directors or even with the community. When individual assets are honored within the context of an explicitly shared identity, there is a wholeness and sense of coherence that was not possible before. When people share identity, they also share their assets, contributing them to the good of the whole, appreciating the assets others bring.

On the other hand, when teacher and students come together and see themselves as separate and isolated entities occupying the same space, they establish a working dynamic that is more like the parallel play of toddlers. They are in the same space, playing in their own separate realms, sometimes even sharing their toys, but never really having meaningful interaction—except when one has something the other wants. And in that moment they are in conflict. In such a relationship, there is no attention to assets, except to consider what the other has that I can use as my own.

98

Generative engagement means that we have come together in collaboration to share our resources, our perspectives. We are unified in our shared identity.

What Matters to Us? Shared Power

The Generative Engagement model uses a definition of power as "the ability to influence." Who has power to influence and who doesn't? How is power assigned or earned? Is power among and between members of the system balanced across time or space? Shared power is about working together, each of us respecting and accepting each others' assets in balanced, equitable collaboration.

The issue of power speaks to what is really important in creating generative relationships. When one person has power over others, there is no path for reciprocal influence. Do I listen to you with a willingness to be informed? Do you hold bias and prejudices that prevent you from considering my assets seriously? Do my decisions consider your wants, needs, and/or assets—or merely my impressions or perspectives of what you want or need? Do your decisions consider mine? That's what we mean when we say that power is balanced. We each come to a relationship with as much willingness to be influenced as to influence. We share power to collaborate without giving up responsibility or accountability.

When certain people in a system have power and others do not, we say that power is out of balance. Those conditions are often set and maintained through an unspoken system of privilege and entitlement. For example, the dominant culture influences events, expectations, rules, and regulations in such a way that others have less power. Even when this imbalance is unconscious and/or unintentional, the potential of the whole is reduced because the time, talents, and other assets of the marginalized are unavailable to the whole. Real collaboration is impossible.

On the other hand, shared power expands and enhances the adaptive capacity of a system. When power is shared in a classroom, teacher and students engage together in joint inquiry, building on each other's' assets to change or influence the disposition of the whole. Shared power does not ask anyone to give up authority or accountability. What it does is ask that those who are decision makers share power; they must allow themselves to be influenced by those who are affected by the decisions. It sets the conditions for leadership and collaboration to emerge where it's needed across the system.

How Do We Connect? Shared Voice

The critical factor in sharing information and other resources lies in how we grant and generate voice. Voice in this sense is our individual or shared agency. It is the essence of who we are and how we express our identity as we engage with each other. These engagements manifest as we speak and listen, act and observe, give and receive. When we grant voice, we listen to others to hear their meaning; we observe without bias; and we receive graciously. When we generate voice, we speak so others can hear and understand what we say; we act in ways that allow them to perceive our meaning; and we give in ways that are timely and considerate. Generative engagements require participants to be constantly vigilant to grant and generate voice simultaneously, and this can only be done when we pay attention to others' assets and needs.

Granting and generating voice is a continuous and simultaneous responsibility of each party in collaboration, whether it is between teacher and student or between the school district and the community. In each exchange, granting and generating voice means that we make decisions about how we express ourselves—verbally and nonverbally—and about how we see or hear others. It means that we give and we take; we speak and we listen. It also means that we stand in inquiry as we seek coherence with those around us.

Time Out for Reflection

*Focus on a relationship that you wish were more collaborative. It might be your relationship with one or more co-workers, or it might be among staff for whom you are responsible. Do a **CDE analysis** of the situation.*

*What are the **containers** that are relevant to all the players? Their roles and job titles? Their shared identity around their work? Gender? Ethnicity? How can you strengthen a **shared container/identity** so they can build on their similarities?*

*What are the **differences** that matter to them? How can you help them focus on differences that are most relevant to their shared work and ignore differences between and among them that don't really matter to the work? How can you **share power around those differences**?*

*What are their current **exchanges**? How can you adjust those exchanges so that they can communicate more clearly and get feedback in a timely way? Considering the Cs, Ds, and Es, what are your options for action? What will be the easiest to accomplish, with the most potential for shifting the conditions? How can you **grant and generate voice** to move your work forward?*

Non-Generative Patterns of Engagement

One way to explore generative engagement is to think about what it is not. Teachers and learners in schools often unintentionally generate non-collaborative patterns of interaction. Sometimes these patterns emerge when people operate on preconceived expectations, focusing on the familiar and ignoring new information.

> *I went to high school in the district where my mom was a central office administrator. I remember the first day I was in high school, I came around the corner and almost ran into the woman who knew my mother and who had taught both my older siblings several years before. Her only comment was, "Here comes trouble, I can see it from here." Turning to her colleague, a new teacher at the school, she explained who I was, not by giving my name, but by describing my family connections. I felt like I didn't have a prayer of having my own persona in the school--I knew I would always be seen through the lens of who these people expected me to be, rather than who I wanted to be.*

> *—School Media Specialist*

Bias robs individuals of voice, and it is often insidious. Without being aware of it, a group of people can be dominated by patterns of expectations about what is acceptable rather than by their own experiences of what works or not. Given the ways patterns get set in a complex adaptive system (CAS), it's easy to see how these patterns then become the culture of the system. Some people are excluded; others are included. Individuals are judged, not by their assets, but by the expectations others have about them. Most of the time these patterns emerge, not because people intentionally set those conditions, but because of historical constraints in the system that shape those patterns.

Think about the non-generative behaviors that emerge at all scales in a system and in multiple ways—from blatant attacks to the unintended, but damaging ways we interact, as exemplified in the story of the media specialist above.

- Bullying
- Abuse of authority
- Prejudice and bias

- Building responses or services for all based on the needs or wants of a few
- Gossip
- Isolation of new and inexperienced teachers
- Withdrawing attention or participation
- Low expectations of non-mainstreamed students
- Over-representation of minorities and males in special education programs.

Think about the ways in which these behaviors limit adaptive capacity as they devalue individual assets and contributions. On the other hand, consider the potential that can be realized through patterns that engage in ways that don't reflect these constraints.

Generative Patterns of Engagement

Generative engagement is about setting conditions that invite people to collaborate with one another in sincere and authentic ways. In generative engagements, participants feel safe enough to bring their assets into the ongoing exchange, knowing that power will be shared and that their voices will matter. Generative patterns emerge when everyone follows the simple rule that is the subject of this chapter: *Recognize and build on assets of self and others.*

Although bullying and privilege mean power in non-generative patterns, generative engagements seek shared power based on individual and group strength and influence. Where prejudice and bias promote one-size-fits-all answers or expectations, generative engagements create responsive, equitable expectations where people work together effectively. Where the only viable response for some was to withdraw and remain silent, generative engagement encourages and celebrates the emergence of multiple and diverse voices in the system to contribute equally to coherence and sustainability. Where fear and intolerance of difference creates separation and exclusion of individuals and groups, generative engagements create safety and opportunities for people to express how they are different from the norm in a group.

Adaptive capacity and generative engagement go hand in hand. Adaptive capacity at multiple scales—the classroom, the school, or the school district—is the flexibility and responsiveness needed for collaboration. One indicator of our adaptive capacity is how well we set conditions that connect people so they can share influence and voice as they move forward.

*We need a program that can help us see differences, and
one that can help us go beyond the training to know how to
respond in any situation that comes up in our school.*
                                            —School Principal

Individuals make choices in every moment to move toward or away
from generative engagements. There is no ultimate place where there will no
longer be challenges around the differences in human systems. This model is
not about avoiding or eliminating difference. This model is about the choices
humans make each moment as they seek to reduce or accommodate the
potential for tension in their systems.

*We had a task force that studied bullying all year, and last
spring, we heard their report and decided how we would
address our bullying problems. We put those expectations in
place, but we haven't seen much improvement because people
are seeing only the grossest examples of bullying. When we
talk about micro-aggressions and subtle forms of bullying,
people get defensive and refuse to talk about it.*
                                            —School Principal

Generative engagement is not about shame or blame. Generative
engagements are about responding to differences in ways that create the
greatest "fit" across the whole system. If we can talk about generative
engagement as a way of life, then people begin to see the more subtle forms
because they have named specifically what they want, and don't have to feel
blamed about what they don't see.

*I think, on our campus, we have learned how to include all the
students—no matter who they are or where they come from.
We celebrate all kinds of diversity, and we invite kids to bring
their background knowledge into the classroom. We try to
take advantage of the diversity so that we can all learn from
one another. But when our kids go to middle school, it's
apparently a very different story. At least that's what we hear
from the kids and their parents.*
                                            —Teacher in Elementary School

This model addresses generative engagements across the scales of
the system. It works as well for interpersonal relationships as it does in a
classroom or at the policy level across a system. People can talk with first
graders about generative engagements, and they can talk with high school
seniors about creating generative engagements. It creates a common language
across the whole system.

When we went to diversity training, we learned about how different cultural responses and practices. We learned all about how we are all different. What we didn't learn was how to behave and respond to each other across those differences.

—Middle School Assistant Principal

This model takes into account each of the questions that emerge about setting the conditions for generative patterns. What do I do to find out more about our shared identity or to amplify those parts we share? How do I allow myself to be influenced by others? How do I influence others without coercion or threat? How do I hear what others are saying and express myself so that they hear me? This model is about knowing how to take action at any moment.

Our students can talk about bias and prejudice in their social studies classes, citing the importance of civil rights or why justice is critical in a society. But some of those same students will get reported for bullying or for racial slurs.

—High School Counselor

Generative engagement goes beyond textbook examples of history and literature, and teaches people how to make choices and decisions in all aspects of their lives. It is not just about race or color or one form of justice. It's about how people treat each other in each moment, how they value assets in others, and how they work together for system sustainability.

Generative Engagements as Adaptive Capacity

Schools are filled with potential conflicts—conflicts that are triggered by differences between and among people. We use generative engagement to create a culture that opens space for people to share their assets, so that they can work with others to contribute to the patterns of the whole. In other words, we use generative engagement to encourage collaboration.

The best news is that improving collaboration does not take a huge intervention. We can move toward collaboration with small actions because issues around identity, power, and voice are interdependent and massively entangled. Shifting one of those three conditions will have an impact on the other two. For instance, when I shift my identity to align with yours, I hear your requests for help and your input in a different way—I am more likely to be influenced by you. At the same time, if I stop to grant you voice—really listen to what you are saying verbally, physically, and behaviorally—I cannot help but know more about you and be influenced in some way by what you say. Any one of these shifts in my own behavior contributes to deeper understanding and opens the door to more powerful collaboration.

When all exchanges across a system can be characterized as generative, the system is more sensitive to its internal and external environments—better able to sense and detect changes, challenges, and opportunities. When generative engagements are the norm in a system, it is more likely to use the broadest range of assets and contributions of each member to respond in productive and sustainable ways. Generative engagements increase the points of contact among people, creating the potential for stronger, more robust collaboration. Generative engagements increase adaptive capacity across scales—among the whole, the part, and the greater whole.

SO WHAT ABOUT COLLABORATION?

In Chapters 3 and 4, we talked about how patterns scale, or emerge across the system, at the whole, in the part, and at the greater whole. Although the language we use in describing and explaining generative engagements points most obviously to person-to-person relationships, the concepts do scale to all levels of the system. Besides considering generative engagement among individuals, we can also consider what has to happen in group or community relationships to establish conditions that are likely to shape generative patterns of engagement, just as it is possible to consider that same issue at the level of policy or legislative action. If school districts are to be places where people recognize and build on assets at the individual, group, and community levels, they will be more successful if they are able to establish generative engagements at all scales. And recognizing and building on assets at all scales will help build adaptive capacity of the system. The system, at all levels, must set the conditions for granting and generating voice. The system, at all levels, must support collaboration and coherence.

Briefly, collaboration will become a part of a system's culture when people follow this simple rule: **Recognize and build on assets of self and others**. There are hundreds of more specific actions that we can take as we try to live out that rule in our particular classroom or office. The following sections offer suggestions for what those specific actions might be.

Shared Identity Supports Collaboration

Groups of students come together in classes. Classes form the school as a whole; schools come together with the operational departments, parents, and other community members to form a district. At each scale what happens to one or the choices that are made by one part of the system have an impact on the whole. At the same time, what happens at one scale of the system has repercussions for parts of the system at other scales. The individual is not separate from his or her environment. Individual decisions and behavior have an impact on the group; group decisions and behavior affect the individual.

As we focus on the larger system, we often see more difference, and we feel less coherent, less comfortable in our work with others. So, as we move beyond face-to-face interactions, we often create boundaries or categories that help us make sense of the world, that help us feel more comfortable. When we talk about "them", we create such a boundary—naming identities we share to distinguish "us" from "them." Sometimes those boundaries separate us (us/them) from others (and we may or may not like that), sometimes boundaries shift and connect us. As circumstances change, those boundaries may change–aligning us with those who were previously them, sometimes in surprising ways. Boundaries sometimes prevent us from seeing each others' assets; sometimes boundaries are formed by the assets that we hold in common.

Affinities, shared experiences, and our communities draw us together into shared identities. Divergent identities may create tension--differences in who we are, how we think, how we feel, how we behave; differences in how we hear and are heard, how we influence and can be influenced, how we relate to each other while we notice (or not) these growing tensions among us. Something you do may provoke a response in me that shifts me from one identity to another, and we suddenly find that who we are together has been disrupted.

Tension--both positive and negative--at all scales of a system emerges from these interactions between the parts of the system and creates the movement from one pattern to another. The tension that emerges across the diverse or oppositional identities creates patterns of separation, distrust or antipathy.

Tension—both positive and negative— at all scales of a system emerges from these interactions between the parts of the system and creates the movement from one pattern to another. The tension that emerges across diverse or oppositional identities creates patterns of separation, distrust, or antipathy. In contrast, the tension that emerges across diversity in a shared identity generates patterns of shared meaning and goals. The strengths and needs I see in a shared identity, I respond to as though they are my own. There are a number of ways that we can increase our awareness of shared identity across scales in a system. (see Table 5.1)

Table 5. 1: Options for action to enhance shared identity

SHARED IDENTITY AT ALL SCALES	
Definition	Identity is how we name our shared similarity in any given relationship.
Options for Action	
Individual	• Ensure individuals see their roles in contributing to collaborations across the district. • Be sure each work group knows how they contribute to the success of the district. • Be sure parents, community members who are not parents, and the business community all know what they can do to support the schools
Group or Community	• Share stories across the system. • Talk about assets or contributions of people or groups at all scales. • Give examples of successes and how collaborations overcame shared challenges. • Talk about how assets and strengths of various groups in the community are similar and how they all contribute to the success of the whole.
Community Policy	• Ensure that system-wide goals are relevant across the system. • Be sure the direction of the whole is clearly articulated and shared with everyone. • Engage people in cross-cultural and multi-representational collaborations. • Teach students what is important in their school and how different classes or grade levels contribute to the whole. • Engage community members to determine district goals and direction; collaborate with them to move toward those goals

These are just some of the ways a school district can set conditions for shared identity across scales in their districts. And these shared stories, goals, and contributions are even more critical in helping individuals and groups understand about sharing power as they build on assets of the system.

Shared Power at All Scales

Sharing power at all scales means that people listen to each other and consider the impact and input of others. Superintendents listen to the community and to their staff and to the students. School boards do the same. Principals, teachers, students pay attention to and consider assets and needs of others as they make their own decisions about their actions. Generative engagements and collaboration depend on that level of influence and openness.

People at all scales can use power or influence to build interest and energy toward system-wide goals. At the same time, they can abuse power by how they limit or diffuse others' influence. Abuse of power can be an intentional action—shutting others out and taking advantage to make decisions that foster benefit to a select few. On the other hand, individuals may not be aware of how they use an imbalance of power, unconsciously acting according to traditional or cultural expectations. Many of us function somewhere in the middle, creating dynamics that are unique to our situations. In any case, generative engagements require that we pay careful attention to how we use power in the system.

At the largest scale, we need to be aware of how societal patterns sometimes grant power to particular groups—males may have been granted more power than females. People of similar cultural backgrounds may exclude others from decision-making or participation because of unquestioned traditions and biases. Age is sometimes privileged over youth. Physical ability and beauty are given greater advantage.

- Students decide who is more or less popular, depending on how their classmates dress, speak, or behave differently. What could be considered cultural assets of one child (speaking more than one language, different range of experiences, different rich cultural heritage) can become liabilities when one group of students decide that being the same is more important than being yourself.

- Teachers sometimes have pre-conceived notions of what to expect from different groups of students, so they make instructional decisions for the whole, rather than being influenced by the assets or needs of individuals.

- When schools or school districts communicate in a limited number of languages or have meetings at one specific time of day, they limit their abilities to be influenced by or collaborate with those who stand outside of those exchanges.

- Schools or school districts that focus only on the cultural celebrations of the dominant culture are, in essence, limiting the influence of other cultures and ignoring their assets.

Table 5.2.: Options for action to share power across the system

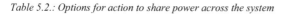

SHARED POWER AT ALL SCALES	
Definition	Across the system, people listen to each other and consider the impact and input of others as decisions are made and as action is taken.
Options for Action	
Individual	• Open difficult conversations to help people realize how positions of privilege inhibit shared power. • Open difficult conversations that invite people to be honest and authentic. • Make everyone aware of the unintentional acts that limit the power of others. • Invite individuals to share their assets and make various contributions.
Group or Community	• Gather input from all sectors in decision making that influences the whole. Find ways to solicit feedback and input in authentic and manageable ways. • Close the loop after gathering input by communicating the rationale for the final decision. • Find ways to tap into groups' cultural assets.
Community Policy	• Ensure that policies create ways for people to influence the system. • Ensure that policies consider influences on all sectors of the community. • Seek policies that create the least constraint appropriate. • Create policies that recognize and celebrate diverse assets throughout the community.

As schools experience greater and greater diversity, it is critical that they make sure they set conditions to influence others without coercion or exclusion, and it is critical that they set conditions that allow all voices to influence system-wide decisions.

Authority—whether granted by position, knowledge, social standing, or other source—can establish a power imbalance. In classrooms, when having power over others is more important than sharing power with others, some students find ways to intimidate or manipulate others as their own way of taking power back. In school systems where top-down mandates drive change efforts, a school staff that feels powerless in the larger scale may literally and figuratively "close its doors" and functionally cut off or limit the district's power in and attempt to find its own voice. A lack of willingness to be influenced is as much an abuse of power as is the use of coercion and oppression to influence others. When you use power over others, you are unable to see and access their assets to engage them in real collaboration.

Generative engagement, as a model, guides action to open possibilities for members of the system to share influence. It invites individuals and groups into moment-by-moment decision- making that creates a dance of action and reaction where individuals observe what is happening around them, consider their own responses and others' contributions, and take intentional steps toward mutual influence and collaboration. It is the systemic recognition and celebration of the assets each person brings to the system, the rules, norms, policies, and procedures that ensure the balance of power across all groups. Table 5.2 lists some general suggestions for sharing power and influence at all scales in a system.

Shared Voice at All Scales

As humans engage with the world, they make choices. In any interaction with others, a person has opportunity to grant voice and opportunity to generate voice. People choose how they listen and speak, observe and act, receive and give in response to their environments. These are the ways they bring their voices into the world, and the ways they damp or amplify other voices. It is how they exhibit their attention to others' assets.

At the system level, granting and generating voice depends on the system-wide conscious intention to create understanding. It is the process of gathering systemic data and making meaning while identifying and questioning possible biases and beliefs. Systems that grant and generate voice don't demand that people fully embrace another's point of view.

110

What they do enforce is that information is used across all scales in a way that allows individuals and groups to see a new perspective or understand something about others.

Table 5.3 represents possible aspects or examples of granting and generating voice at multiple scales across a school system.

Table 5.3: Options for action to grant and generate voice

	SHARED VOICE AT ALL SCALES		
	Speak and Listen	**Act and Observe**	**Give and Receive**
Definition	• Speak into the other's listening • Listen to what is said & not said • Be open to hearing & accepting what others say	• Behave according to social & cultural patterns of those with whom you engage • See others in light of their own social patterns	• Give according to your own & others' needs • Receive with grace • Remain open
	OPTIONS FOR ACTION		
Individual	• Engage in mutual, purposeful conversation • Maintain open dialogue • Seek shared meaning • Bring whole self to interaction	• Observe and use accepted social patterns • Participate in and across affinity groups • Understand and respect multiple cultures	• Share resources (time, energy, information, etc.) • Give and receive, relying on good intention • Honor self and others
Group or Community	• Share information transparently • Seek and consider input from all • Engage others in planning • Honor contributions	• Evaluate with shared criteria • Amplify & damp exchanges according to community need • Connect across groups • Respect boundaries	• Offer & accept feedback and input • Share the work of the community
Community Policy	• Share expectations • Design effective feedback loops • Listen/consider feedback from all groups • Engage across language and culture differences	• Clarify and observe community & cultural expectations • Consider multiple perspectives in • Share rationale and considerations once decision is made	• Solicit input, feedback & contributions according to need & ability • Honor contributions

Generative Patterns at Scale

Whether we focus on the level of the local district, the state agency, or the federal Department of Education, policies and procedures, regulations, and expectations that emerge from generative engagements will increase the chances that emergent patterns of education will engage the assets of individuals and groups across the country. Students and teachers, unions and management, parents and school district will pool their time and talents in reciprocal relationships that benefit all. Each person will engage in authentic work that adds meaning to their lives. Across the system, each individual will experience the justice of having equal access to the goods and services, benefits and opportunities of the schools that serve them. Table 5.4 reflects some examples of how the three patterns of generative engagement can play out across a number of scales.

Table 5.4: Patterns of Generative Engagement across the system.

	RECIPROCITY	AUTHENTICITY	JUSTICE
Teachers & Learners as partners	Learning partners recognize and honor contributions in the classroom	Teachers and learners own their limitations and skills Teachers and learners engage in work that has personal meaning and interest	Individuals grant and generate voice, engaging fully in learning and synergy of relationship
Teacher & Parent partnerships	Individuals share their contributions and recognize contributions of others. Individual needs are known and honored	Each person owns his/her limitations and skills in serving diverse needs of children Parents and teachers share common goals for students	Parents and teachers connect with each other to understand students' progress and learning
Staff as partners in learning	Staff members share information, insights, and skills to create fuller learning experiences	Staff members share their own needs and strengths in interactions with others	Staff members treat each other with respect, afford each other opportunities to participate in greater whole.
Districts & Unions as partners	Both commit to common goals and their shared and interdependent roles	Relationship is characterized by transparency and open dialogue about concerns and interests	Each group promotes fair treatment and respect for the other and for members whom they both serve
District & Agencies as partners	Both recognize and use strengths and benefits of others to contribute to children's learning.	Both groups are clear about the relationships of their roles and their ability to engage in partnerships for the benefit of students	Groups work together to assure students have equal access to opportunities and feedback in the system.
State & Federal generative engagements		Federal and state expectations, establish regulations for local support and service rather than maintaining their traditional role to mandate and monitor local compliance	Federal and state activities recognize and consider the needs and voice of all groups Regulations fulfill the expectation for equal access to the resources of the system

NOW WHAT? LEVERAGE ASSETS FOR ADAPTIVE CAPACITY

At the heart of generative engagement is the realization that we each bring assets to any collaborative relationship:

- If we are to **share identity**, we need to pay attention to the assets of those who stand with us.

- If we are to **share power and influence**, we need to know what others offer and what they want from our reciprocal relationships.

- If we are to **grant or generate voice**, we must know who others are and what they bring to the relationships.

If people throughout the system follow **focus on assets**, generative patterns like reciprocity, authenticity, and justice will emerge. But the rule, "Focus on assets" can easily become an empty platitude. What kinds of assets are we looking for? How do those assets work in complex systems? How do we leverage those assets in ourselves and others?

In research with the North Star of Texas Writing Project, Leslie and her colleagues identified categories of assets—resources that students bring to the teaching/learning relationship. After a year of collaborating with middle and high school teachers who had been identified as particularly responsive to the strengths and needs of English learners, the research team noticed that these teachers focused on certain resources in their students (Wickstrom, Patterson, and Araujo, 2011). The researchers named four categories of assets that offer a point of entry and access for teachers, starting places for building and strengthening student learning. By thinking about specific categories of assets, teachers can begin to think about how to set conditions that will help students build on those strengths. Here are the categories of assets that were important to these teachers:

- Social and cultural resources (funds of knowledge and support networks)
- Knowledge about language (especially their heritage languages)
- Meaning-making and problem-solving strategies
- Academic content knowledge.

Of course, these are the kinds of strengths teachers might look for when they first meet their students at the beginning of the school year, but these are also areas of instructional goals and objectives. For example, the teachers in this study built on the social and cultural resources that each student brought, but they also planned instructional experiences to expand the students' knowledge and skills related to each of these categories.

It occurs to us that these categories might well work at other scales of the system, naming system assets that are necessary at the whole, part, and greater whole. Whether it is at the local, state, or national level, systems that possess these assets have a better chance of supporting students in the acquisition and use of these assets. Table 5.5 on the following page helps to explore ways these assets could be used to build on the strengths and needs of students and staff in our schools.

When we follow the simple rule, *Recognize and build on assets of self and others*, we opt for generative engagement. We open possibilities for honest dialogue and collaborative work. Each agent in the system focuses on strengths, not deficits. Each emerging challenge is seen through multiple perspectives. Those complex perspectives suggest a wide range of promising options for action. Each opportunity can be assessed for its benefit across the whole of the system. Generative engagements clearly build collective capacity (Fullan, 2010), and our collective work is clearly more than the sum of its parts.

Year after year, innovative and hard-working educators face persistent challenges—challenges that require innovative, yet risky approaches. They face resistance to new and unfamiliar practices, no matter how promising. And they face situations where long-standing differences in opinions, background, values, beliefs, experiences make "shared understanding" seem like an impossible dream. In the schools where we have worked, this simple rule about focusing on assets has been foundational. Because it helps us stand in inquiry, about ourselves and others, this simple rule enables and sustains other simple, yet radical assumptions about how people can collaborate to build adaptive capacity to sustain the systems where they live, work, and play.

Table 5.5: Categories of assets that can leverage adaptive capacity at the whole, the part, and the greater whole.

	INDIVIDUAL-LEVEL ASSETS	SYSTEM-LEVEL ASSETS
Social and Cultural Capital	Social skills for collaboration Rich understanding of their own cultures Willingness to stand in inquiry Appreciation for cultural diversity	Ability to value, access, and enhance the rich wealth of social and cultural capital that makes up the tapestry of schools at whatever scale
Linguistic Knowledge	Skills to learn in one's original language Skills to learn in the language of the community Linguistic skills to meet the demands of academic settings Linguistic understanding to be fluent in variety of social, academic, and work settings Ability to grant and generate voice at the individual and group level	Processes and structures that support an openness to diverse range of languages Ability to generate and grant voice to those they serve
Meaning Making & Decision Making Strategies	Ability to make meaning of the world around them Skilled at problem solving in myriad situations Ability to think about their own thinking--to know how they make meaning and solve problems	Expectations, processes, and structures that invite and support an inquiry stance through Adaptive Action Adaptive capacity to ensure sustainable services across economic, social, cultural and technological turbulence of today's landscape
Content Knowledge	Basic mastery of content knowledge Ability to use their knowledge to generate greater understanding through problem-solving and creativity Ability to take an active role in strengthening their repertoire of responses in and out of school	Ability to ensure that students go beyond memorization and facts, to problem solving and creativity Ability to focus on those aims of academic content knowledge will create successful citizens of the future

A Focus on Assets Can Build Innovation

When a system (or an individual) focuses its assets—its energy and resources—on seeing and understanding the dynamics that create its most challenging patterns, people share their perspectives and insights, building new ways of seeing the world. Innovative solutions to those challenges will become apparent. When generative engagements invite people to bring their assets together in shared and reciprocal problem solving, local innovations can create solutions that address system-wide concerns. In the same way, major policy moves that acknowledge assets will enable educators to build on students' strengths and will position everyone to move forward, regardless of the risks they see in the innovative solutions.

A Focus on Assets Can Overcome Resistance and Conflict

When we talk to educators about their sticky issues, we hear story after story of resistance among colleagues, parents, and the larger community. In a school system, promising innovations are often sabotaged by individuals who dig in their heels and refuse to consider anything new or different. In complex systems, resistance emerges from incoherence, from friction between parts of the greater whole. When parts of the greater whole work at cross purposes, tension builds and the energy of the system is spent tending that tension rather than in adapting to changes within and outside the system. Resistance is a pattern characterized chiefly by conflict among the parts of the whole that results from levels of constraint that hold unhealthy levels of tension in the system.

When the agents in a system are over-constrained, they are unable to respond to each other or to their environment in healthy or sustainable ways. Prescriptive reading programs, best practices that require strict fidelity, and mandated, high-stakes testing programs constrain educational systems in ways that prevent or limit collaboration for adaptation and response to individual assets and local context. Teachers and others inside the system resist when they are so constrained that they are unable to respond.

At the other end of the spectrum, systems that are under-constrained also generate patterns of resistance and conflict. In school systems where there is no real coherence in program or shared expectations for student or staff performance, conflict and resistance emerge as people compete for limited resources and attention. Students across the district are treated in inequitable ways as practices across the whole come to reflect only local concerns.

Partisan differences drive decisions according to local political needs rather than according to systemic needs for collaboration and sustainability.

When individuals and groups across the system follow this simple rule, always focusing on assets, they come to see themselves as viable contributors to the whole. When they stand with others to influence the patterns of the whole and when they know their voices are heard in the chorus of the whole, they experience the constraints of the system as supportive and encouraging. This one picture of generative engagement and belief in the students' assets in a high school classroom illustrates this point.

> *Well, I get very honest with my kids. I tell them that my job is to not tell you what the answer is. My job is to help you think and to help you formulate your own analysis and your own questions and you're probably going to be frustrated with me because I'm not going to, I'm not going to sit here and tell you what the answer is or this is what you need to know and you're going to have to decide what's important to you. You're going to have to decide the solutions to the questions and what evidence you're going to use to support your claims. And I often run into kids who are frustrated with that because that's a departure from the structures they've experienced before. There's a tremendous amount of frustration. I've actually had kids tell me well, you don't know how to teach. And so I ask them what do you mean by that? And they'll just tell me well, you're supposed to be up there and tell me what I need to write down. And so we have a conversation about how what that means in terms of power, what that means in terms of value, what is valued? And I don't always get kids to see that, you know, but I try to stick to that commitment so that over time, they see themselves as important, that their thoughts have value, that what they think matters—that they're capable of deep, critical thinking.*
> —*Secondary Teacher*

A focus on assets through generative engagement can also help campus teams to move forward as the team itself recognizes the value of constraints and their own efficacy to contribute to the whole.

> *We've been a team on this campus for three years now. And my principal is really supportive of our learning, and we're supportive of hers . . . So there's a lot of give and take. We are very supportive of one another, and I think that has moved the school forward. . . . And one shift that helped us was the whole idea of shared voice and the*

ability to influence one another through generative engagement. I didn't feel like we were having generative engagement before, but we are moving forward in that. . . For our dialogue, it's helped us a lot.

–Elementary Instructional Coach

Conflict and resistance dissipate as people acknowledge strengths in one another and in the system and as they engage in generative ways to solve their shared challenges and maximize their shared opportunities.

A Focus on Assets Builds System-wide Energy

Generative Engagement is not a silver bullet that will dispel the challenges of difference overnight. Patterns of generative engagement do not create a Utopia where everything is wonderful, and there are no more challenges. When there is a system-wide commitment to creating generative engagements—a commitment to focus on assets—people are supported in making moment-by-moment choices that set the conditions for generative patterns. The system's energy at any one point becomes the catalyst for choosing individual and group action in the next moment. Any one of those choices, whether by an individual, a group, or the district as a whole, will either move the system toward more generative patterns or away from generative patterns. It's not an event, and it does not occur in a vacuum. Here is how an elementary teacher described this shift at his campus:

> *We are at a point where no teacher goes and teaches unless we all plan together, and that's a big deal. Now that's starting as a pattern to go into other strategies that we use. . . So that's a big, big shift, especially for our school because we're noticing that the resistance level is far less. Our staff meetings are all instructional rather than business-oriented because there's this common goal that we're all trying to reach. So that was cool. I don't know if [my principal] talked about this but I was thinking about my grade level and the whole school, the whole idea of our generative learning, the adaptive action cycle, the what, the so what and the now what, that's kind of the course we've taken with every single thing that we've done at [my site]. About a year and a half ago, we all seemed to be teaching in our own classrooms with our own ideas about what is, what's going to make kids successful. We never opened our rooms to anybody. So thanks to the formation of the*

118

Instructional Leadership Team here, paralleled by the
HSD, we were able to approach this better and now we .
. . have discussions around strategies that we use and
develop some common agreements . . . Now what? Now
we are in a better position. We are doing safe practice.
We are opening classrooms to each other. It's not so
much evaluative. It's there is my colleague, come by and
tell me how this student is behaving while I'm teaching
or come by and tell me whether I'm reaching out to my
ELL kids or not. So it's more for feedback and sort of the
safe practice, which we did not have earlier. So the
whole idea of where were we, where are we going, you
know it's just the adaptive action cycles that seem to be
working for us really well.

–Elementary Teacher

This transformation in how people interact and move forward together happens each moment in the context of the forces and opportunities in the system. Generative engagements recognize and build on individual, social, and cultural assets to build strong and sustainable patterns of teaching and learning.

NOW WHAT? USE THESE RESOURCES TO LEARN MORE

Pierce, C. M., Carew, J. V., Pierce-Gonzalez & Wills, D. (1977). *An Experiment in Racism: TV Commercials. Education and Urban Society, 10*, 1, 61–87.

Sue, D. W.; Capodilupo, Christina M.; Torino, G. C.; Bucceri, J. M.; Holder, A. M. B.; Nadal, K. L.; Esquilin, M. Racial microaggressions in everyday life: Implications for clinical practice. *American Psychologist, 62*, 271-286.

Hooks, B. (2009). *Teaching critical thinking: Practical wisdom.* New York: Routledge.

The project of the southern poverty law center. Retrieved Feb 2013 from http://www.tolerance.org/

Rethinking schools. Retrieved Feb, 2013 from http://www.rethinkingschools.org/

CHAPTER 6:
True and Useful

Educational ideologies, structures, and practices in the United States have typically assumed a separation between theory and practice. From a human systems dynamics perspective, such a distinction is not possible. To build coherence in a complex system, the integration of theory and practice must be seamless—we learn by doing, and we teach by doing——in shared cycles of action and inquiry. This chapter explains how to integrate theory and practice so that we can work toward coherence in our teaching and learning throughout schools systems.

Central Challenge	Achieve Coherence
Simple Rule	Seek the true and the useful.
Concepts, Methods, and Models	• Praxis • Four Truths • Architectural Model
Guiding Questions	• What do we mean by "true and useful"? • What is praxis? • So how do we know what is true? • So how do we build coherence in schools? • Now what? Build coherence for Adaptive Capacity. • Now what? Use these resources to learn more.

Each day educators are deluged by problems——both routine and urgent. These problems pull them in many directions at once; too often their work is fragmented, not at all coherent or focused. The first challenge is to set priorities. Where to begin? One HSD practitioner shares his perspective:

The reality is we have to focus on what we can control, I can't spend any second of my day talking about the true and useless. So much of our talk is about things we can't control, like "but if the parents would only take care of business." That conversation may be true, but it's useless. So the minute the conversation goes there, I say, "That may be true about the students' families, but I can't spend any more time on trying to solve something that's out of my control. Right now we need to concentrate on the true and useful and not the true and useless. And I have begun saying things like that with the parents, the staff members, and kids——in all my interactions. What I'm thinking now is about what we can do together. And this has been excellent for me.

—Elementary School Principal

As we face these daily challenges, we are flooded with theories, frameworks, standards, strategies, programs, tools, approaches, methodologies——most of which promise that the more we standardize our work, the less fragmented we will be, and the more efficient and effective the results. There is no shortage of people and products offering to rescue us. Silver bullets abound! This chapter offers a simple but potentially life-saving rule to help us set priorities and to achieve coherence:

Seek the true and the useful.

This rule is not about choosing between two unrelated alternatives—on the one hand, what we know to be true, and on the other the tools and strategies we find useful. It's about focusing on what we know to be BOTH true and useful. Everything else falls away. This simple rule is about closing those persistent theory-to-practice gaps that eternally plague school reformers. It's about tapping the driving passion that teachers and learners have for creative problem solving. At its root, this simple rule is about a seamless and generative integration of what we know and what we do. When agents in a complex adaptive system (CAS) consistently make connections and take action about what they know to be true and what their experience tells them works, coherent patterns emerge at the whole, the part, and the greater whole.

122

WHAT DO WE MEAN BY "TRUE AND USEFUL"?

When we bring together our knowledge (theory) and our experiences (practice), we stand a better chance of coming up with action-oriented solutions. At least we come up with options for Adaptive Action—the options may not completely solve our problems, but we can move toward solutions. And, as we have pointed out repeatedly, Adaptive Action——because it is iterative and responsive——can build more generative and sustainable systems. Figure 6.1 represents that emergent process.

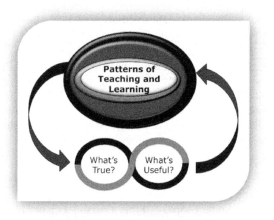

Figure 6.1: Emergence of true and useful patterns. As insights and experience that are both true and useful interact, patterns of generative teaching/learning emerge.

Time Out for Reflection

Think about the last time you and your colleagues looked at test score reports. Those reports are 'true' but of what 'use' are they? Are they useful for predicting individual performance? For planning instruction for individuals? For groups? For teacher evaluation? How can we approach test scores so that they are both true and useful?

Not only does this approach help the adults in school systems focus and move forward, it can also be helpful to students. One fifth grade teacher says that "true and useful" became a part of the daily discourse in his classroom:

My kids say what's true and useful in class. My kids will
ask themselves, "Well, is this something true and useful
that will contribute to the class?" They understand it.

—Elementary Teacher

WHAT IS PRAXIS?

Figure 6.1 suggests that as professionals, we continually integrate what seems true with what seems useful. That interaction generates patterns that can propel our work forward toward particular insights and solutions to problems of practice. Let's drill down a bit into those two sources of knowledge. "Truth" is our theoretical knowledge—our definitions, descriptions, and explanations about a particular phenomenon. "Useful" refers to our practical experience—our skills, strategies, and our sense of whether or not these help us solve problems in the "real" world. These are two ways of knowing about the world, and they are often thought of as separate—in what philosophers call a dualism. We've already pointed out that in HSD, we think of them as integrated—two dimensions of our knowledge. We think this applies in all areas of our lives, but for now, let's focus on our professional knowing.

As professionals, we reflect on what we already know about how and why teaching and learning work the way they do—our theoretical knowledge. Some people call this a personal theory base or mental model. For example, first-grade teachers have a theory base about what it means to "read" that influences how they support beginning readers. No matter what their curriculum or reading program suggests, individual teachers will make decisions that fit what they understand to be true about learning to read.

We also reflect on our practical experiences—what works and what doesn't. Think back to the explanation of patterns in Chapter 4. We notice and name emergent patterns in our practical experiences. Those patterns guide our next steps as we act on what we know and as we learn even more. Think about how those first-grade teachers look for patterns; they know what has always worked to help their students learn to read, and their practical experiences inform what they do to support their beginning readers. They combine their theories about reading with their practical experiences about what works in their classrooms.

This dynamic and emergent interaction between our theory base and practice is called "praxis." The word "praxis" comes from Greek and Latin roots and means, literally, "doing." The term has been used by theorists like Marx and Freire to refer to a creative and integrative approach to thoughtful, deliberate action—the integration of theory and practice. Freire, in particular, claims that humans are essentially "unfinished" and that we are driven, through praxis, to make sense of the world and to exercise our agency to change the world for the better. For Freire and other critical educators, a "better" world is one where marginalized and oppressed people, through praxis, make a difference for themselves and for others (Freire, 1970; Freire and Macedo, 1998). We are using "praxis" in the same sense—as a creative, hopeful, and liberating integration of theory and practice.

Emerging praxis shapes further inquiry, reflection, and action. Experience and ideas form system-wide patterns in our praxis. Emerging patterns constrain subsequent practical decisions and thoughts. Figure

6.2 is a model of this ongoing, recursive, complex, and adaptive process.

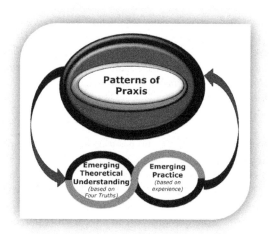

Figure 6.2: Praxis emerging in a complex adaptive system. Praxis emerges in a generative teaching/learning system as agents act on what they see as both true and useful.

Educators value "research-based practice" of course, but this graphic representation helps us move beyond talking about "research-based practice" as an expectation imposed on teachers. Rather, this model focuses on the teacher as an agent and a meaning-maker. Teachers consider research findings as a part of what is true, and research certainly influences their praxis. But it's not just about what the experts say will work; it's about taking the research findings from outside the classroom and integrating those with their practical experiences to build their informed decisions—their praxis. Here is how this picture of praxis helped a literacy coach:

> *Our district-wide coach's team was working on how to support the teachers who were new to guided reading. We were trying to figure out what the teachers needed to create this document that would help guide their work. I wish I had known about this image of praxis. A lot of times, the teachers I work with focus on their practice but don't know why a particular practice works. It's just not enough theory. I know there's the need for both, but what teachers need is a fluid movement back and forth—sometimes theory, sometimes practice. With teachers, I was really trying hard to say things like, "Well, that's true in our practice, but what does theory tell us?" And I think I found it frustrating because I didn't have the verbiage to really create that dialogue. I wasn't sure what I was trying to get at. A lot of times I hear things like, "I've taught for 20 years so. . ." and I want to say, "That's great. But is that still true for now—with today's kids?" So this praxis model will help me have that theory-to-practice conversation with teachers.*

> *—Elementary Literacy Coach*

The divide between theory and practice has created many crises in educational policy over the past decade. For example, in 1998, California voters approved Proposition 227, an attempt to end bilingual education in public schools. The implementation of this law fell primarily on classroom teachers, who were immediately expected to change their instructional practices with English learners. Many teachers were bilingual teachers in May, 1998, and English-only teachers the next fall. The policy changed, and practices were expected to change immediately, with no regard for teachers' understandings about what was true or useful.

Stritikus (2003) documented one teacher's experience trying to respond to this dramatic policy change. Celia (pseudonym) was a first-grade teacher in a small rural district. She was born in Mexico and moved with her family to California as an infant, which meant that she had linguistic and cultural experiences similar to those of her students. Her family spoke primarily Spanish at home, and her parents had taught her to read in Spanish. Although she was never involved in a formal bilingual education program, she did grow up with access to both Spanish and

English. She began teaching in a bilingual classroom, where her instruction focused on Spanish language and literacy development. It would seem that this approach would have matched Celia's praxis. It was grounded in both Celia's theory (what she learned in her teacher education program) and her practice (her experiences as an English learner).

However, after the passage of Proposition 227 in California, when the district switched to a tightly controlled, teacher-directed, English-only approach, Celia was not bothered by the change, although it would seem to contradict her previous approach. She was cautiously optimistic, citing her successful experiences in what she remembered as something like the English-immersion approach that she was being asked to implement. So she threw herself into trying to implement the new program, assuming that what the experts recommended would work with her students. By February, however, she was questioning whether the absolute insistence on English was the most useful practice for her students. She began making time to read to the children in Spanish, and she was encouraging students to use their knowledge about their first language to improve their use of English. These practices, of course, were in direct opposition to Proposition 227 and to the district-mandated instructional program.

In Celia's story, we see that actual implementation of education policy in a real classroom is mediated by the teacher's praxis. We also see that Celia's ongoing negotiation between "theory" and "practice" are influenced in complex and unpredictable ways by her own biography, by the policy itself, by her campus contexts, and (perhaps most powerfully) by her students' responses. This integration of theory ("what we know should work") with practice ("what we have seen work") is typical of how educators try to integrate the true with the useful.

SO HOW DO WE KNOW WHAT IS TRUE?

What is true, after all? Questions about the nature of truth, of course, have challenged humankind for centuries. So we are not attempting a comprehensive philosophical discussion, and we are not going to settle those ongoing debates about the nature of truth in the next few paragraphs. But we have found a way to think about how we decide what is true (and useful) and what is not. This tool helps us move forward through potential conflicts with colleagues, with students, and with stakeholders. We call it "The Four Truths."

In schools, we seldom have time for philosophical discussions because we are always putting out big and little fires. And we are usually trying to sort through multiple perspectives and opinions on what to do next, whether to use a bucket or call in the fire brigade. When we find ourselves in confrontations about how to solve these pressing problems, it is sometimes useful to think more deeply about what each person in the situation claims to be "true." As human beings, we make particular truth claims about the world, and then those truths become the basis for our actions. Imagine a campus leadership team trying to decide whether or not to implement a requirement that students wear uniforms.

Here are some examples of truth claims we might hear:

- Uniforms build shared identity and pride in the school.
- Uniforms squelch individual creativity and identity.
- Uniforms make the differences between affluent and non-affluent kids less noticeable.
- Uniforms avoid conflicts about dress code violations.
- Our community would reject (would welcome) uniforms.
- Uniforms make the campus feel like a military academy, and I like that.
- Uniforms make the campus feel like a military academy, and I hate that.

How can all these contradictory and overlapping claims be integrated and resolved? Which are more compelling? Which are grounded in evidence? How can we move forward with a decision that will be both true and useful?

Notice that each claim is based on a particular kind of knowledge or experience. For centuries, rhetoricians have pointed to different kinds of evidence—*logos, pathos,* and *ethos.* In human systems dynamics, the **Four Truths** are similar to those categories. More specifically, HSD has adapted concepts from the German philosopher Jurgen Habermas (1984; 1987). He describes three kinds of claims about "truth": objective; normative; and subjective. He calls these categories "ontological realms"—or realms relating to what we see as "real." In HSD, we call them kinds of "truth," and we add a fourth truth, which relates to what Habermas calls "intersubjectivity." We call the fourth truth "complex truth." We see no hierarchy; they each have equal potential to influence our knowledge and action.

Objective Truth Claims

An objective truth claim is grounded in shared data or experience. If multiple people observe an event and make the same claim about what is true, that is an "objective" truth. In other words, multiple people have access to an objective truth. Here are some examples of objective truths that we hear in schools:

- The third graders' reading comprehension scores are 8% better this year than last year's third graders' scores.
- The state legislature just passed a mandate for end-of-course examinations for core subject areas in high school.
- In the last month, ten parents have complained that they do not have enough input into decisions about the school calendar.
- The local newspaper has published only one positive report about what is happening in the local school district in the last six months.

In some contexts, people seem to think that "objective" claims are more "true" than other kinds of information. Perhaps that is because they are grounded in evidence or are associated with scientific research. In fact, No Child Left Behind and other recent policy documents have emphasized the use of "scientific research" or "evidence-based programs" because of the assumptions that only objective truth can and should guide decisions in schools. We do not, however, see objective truth as more "true" than the other kinds of truth; we simply acknowledge that it comes from a different source. Objective truth is certainly an essential consideration as we are looking for true and useful ways to put out our fires. An objective truth claim takes its power from the fact that multiple people have access to the same evidence and make the same claim. Because of incontrovertible evidence, we can trust that objective truth gives us information about how the world works.

Subjective Truth Claims

In contrast to objective truths, subjective truth claims are grounded in a single person's experience. We typically think of them as feelings, attitudes, perceptions, or beliefs although they are often stated as absolute truths. These claims cannot be challenged because the person making the claim is the only one who has access to that reality. Here are some subjective truths that we might hear in schools:

- I am worried about this year's third-grade class and their reading scores.
- Parents always complain when school policy interferes with family vacations.
- I don't think this community values education.

- These students (or teachers or parents) simply don't care; that's all there is to it.
- We have the best students (or teachers or parents) in the district.
- We are doing the best we can, given our constraints.

In some contexts, subjective truth claims are either ignored or dismissed. The word "subjective" is often used derogatorily, as if personal feelings and attitudes are not significant and should not be considered. We disagree. We agree, instead, with the adage, "perception IS reality." Counselors will tell us how important it is for us to learn to acknowledge and express our feelings——to be in touch with our emotional reality. The importance of these subjective truths scale to larger systems because the perceptions or the subjective realities of everyone in schools will influence how they work and play together. Those realities influence how we teach and learn. We cannot dismiss subjective truths and still hope to move forward toward more generative teaching/learning in schools. We simply need to acknowledge that subjective truths are one kind of truth among others that are equally "true" and sometimes useful.

Normative Truth Claims

Normative claims are grounded in agreements (both explicit and implicit) among members of a community. Normative truths can emerge among families, classrooms, school district leadership teams, neighborhoods, faith communities, or any functional group. These are sometimes framed as cultural norms, values, or beliefs. They may be influenced by social expectations or unspoken rules. They have powerful effect, even if the group is a temporary one. In other words, sometimes these truths are influenced by peer pressure. Here are some normative truths that we might hear in schools:

- We tend to act as if writing instruction is only important at the grades when students take the state test.
- Of course, ninth-grade students should be able to write a literary analysis about *Romeo and Juliet*.
- On this campus, we treat parents as "stake-holders" so we try to listen to their input about all our policy issues.
- Around here, we don't talk to the press unless we have to.
- We are doing the best we can, given our constraints.

Complex Truth Claims

Of course, any conversation is a mash-up of these three kinds of truths. We mix and match them as we advance our positions or explain our decisions. Usually we speak without thinking about why we consider each one to be true. In HSD, we argue that our conversations (and confrontations) will be more generative when we think about which truth(s) we are claiming. As we listen to others, we should think about whether they are making objective, subjective, or normative truth claims. As we think about their kind of truth we can respond in more open and generative ways. Together, we can see our areas of agreement and use those as springboards to new insights and options for action. Each kind of truth has its place, and each one should guide our thinking and our actions in appropriate ways.

When we fail to make distinctions among these claims and how they function in particular situations, conflicts and contradictions show up. For example, I might make a subjective claim and think it is objective. I might be offended that others don't accept my subjective truth as an absolute truth, valid for everyone. What is "true" for me should be "true" for everyone, right?

Or I might hear a colleague make an objective claim about third graders' reading comprehension. If I am not aware of her supporting evidence, I could treat it as an unsupported opinion, or subjective truth. I would then dismiss it because I don't see it as a statement of objective truth.

Or, as a campus community, we might assume that our normative truth (for example that all ninth graders should read *Romeo and Juliet*) is an objective truth for all ninth graders everywhere. We would criticize the middle school teachers if ninth graders come to our campus without the "right" background knowledge and reading skills to make sense of the play.

Anyone who has worked in schools can come up with dozens of similar examples. These examples illustrate how messy our discussions about important policy and instructional decisions can be. This is complex business, primarily because multiple, contradictory truth claims might be expressed to address any single issue. The Four Truths help us sort through these contradictions. They help us see patterns in our discourse. Our dialogue can be much more productive if we think about each claim that's made and why we think that it is true.

"Complex truth" assumes that we can imagine how each one of the first three truths might function in a particular conversation. The complex truth takes the position (or combination of positions) that is true, but also the most useful. It is —a position that can move the conversation, the learning, or the work forward. For example, we might foreground someone's subjective truth when the issue prompts a strong emotional reaction. We might foreground an objective truth (with the empirical evidence that supports it) as we are considering a policy change. We might foreground a normative truth when our shared beliefs or identities are at stake. The fourth truth, complex truth, is about flexibility and adaptability. Searching for the complex truth requires generative learning, but it also sets the conditions for people to sustain their generative teaching/learning over time. The complex truth is essentially a way of seeing and naming the true and the useful.

If everyone knows about the Four Truths, we can explicitly foreground one truth at a time. This way, we give it more importance in a particular situation at a particular moment, so we move the other potential truth claims to the background. This reduces the tension and the potential for conflict or incoherence. As we think or talk about a controversial issue, we can learn how to take up one truth and then another. We can explore all sides of the issue, looking for patterns to make sense (and take action) either individually or collectively. When we really listen to others, we try to understand their truth claims by empathizing with their subjective truths, examining the supporting evidence for their objective truths, and clarifying shared values underlying their normative truths.

If our colleagues are not aware of the Four Truths, we might use these statements to help the group consider multiple perspectives on truth.

- So what kind of evidence (or data) do we have to back up what we are saying?

- Do you think that what you just said is true for all of us, or is that your personal experience?

- I've noticed that, on this campus, we seem to be operating as if that is true. I wonder if people on other campuses would agree with us.

Figure 6.3 represents the Four Truths as a specific model or method that helps people see, understand, and influence patterns in complex adaptive systems. In fact, we might think of the Four Truths as patterns of expression for our individual and collective understandings and experiences of reality. The right truth for each situation is defined by fit. The right truth is the one that is most appropriate, given all we know about the challenges, the players, and their goals in that situation. We select the claim that is most true and useful in that particular time and place. This sometimes calls for compromise; sometimes for negotiation and consensus-building. Open and honest flexibility around these truths helps us move our work forward. It helps us make appropriate and adaptive decisions as each challenge shows up.

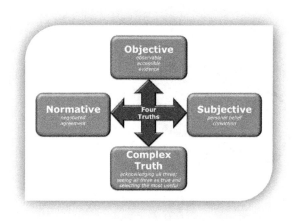

Figure 6. 3: The Four Truths. Our claims about what is true and useful are grounded in one or more of these four kinds of truth.

Here's a story about how the Four Truths facilitated conversations on an elementary campus:

> *I'm using the "Four Truths" to have conversations about administrative mandates that cause negative feelings among teachers. By noticing whether we are talking about a subjective truth or an objective truth, we are getting to the root of why they have this belief. For example, we can say, "What are you saying?" What evidence makes you feel that way?" So for example, some of the teachers really didn't like the walk-throughs. They said, "They (administrators) are just judging us." I said, "Oh really? What has actually happened that made you feel that way? I'm trying to remember when someone has actually received negative consequences after a walk-through. Is this an objective truth?" Together we realize, just by*

133

*talking about those kinds of truth, that we haven't, in fact,
been judged because of these walk-throughs. We still may
have our subjective negative feelings, but we have to
acknowledge that what some of the teachers were saying
was not an objective truth.*

—*Instructional Coach*

This story shows how, as complex adaptive agents in complex
adaptive school systems, we can use the Four Truths as a mental model
for clarifying the source of our truth claims.

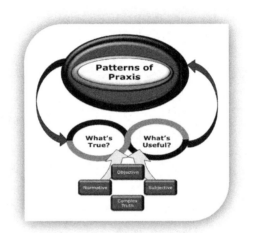

*Figure 6.4: Generative teaching/learning cycle. Patterns of
praxis emerge from a consideration of the true and the useful,
which is grounded in one or more of the Four Truths.*

colleagues ... ... larged
issues that are at the heart of school transformation. Models are about what
is true; methods are about what is useful. The Four Truths give us both a
model and a method.

SO HOW DO WE BUILD COHERENCE IN SCHOOLS?

With all those urgent and divergent challenges we mentioned at
the beginning of this chapter, it is no wonder that educators' work has
become fragmented. In efforts to gain control of this chaos, educators and
policy-makers have looked to policies and programs that promise
"standardization," "fidelity of implementation" and "best practice."
Politicians claim that math achievement will increase if we simply
standardize the curriculum. Commercial programs promise higher test
scores if their recommendations are implemented with fidelity. Flashy

brochures describe how this or that in-service program focuses on best practice. As HSD practitioners, we see those promises as signs of an understandable desire to build coherence across the system. But we also think that such approaches are based on a misguided and ultimately disastrous approach to school reform.

Early in the days of the industrial revolution, policy makers began to see the need to create structures to ensure efficiency and productivity. As the population increased, as factories grew and as people moved to the cities, leaders had to find a way to manage larger and larger organizations. Bureaucracies emerged. The assembly line, IQ tests, teacher certification, and the U.S. Department of Education all grew out of this need to organize and manage huge tasks efficiently. The current wave of school reform follows a similar rationale, using standards, tests, funding incentives, and accountability measures as bureaucratic structures to increase efficiency and productivity. Of course, structure is necessary in any system. Large organizations need structure to make processes and procedures more predictable and efficient, but we think there are alternatives to structures that attempt to standardize the complex and unpredictable processes of teaching and learning.

Our understanding of classrooms and schools as complex adaptive systems means that each learner, each classroom, and each campus is absolutely unique. Common phrases like "fidelity of implementation" and "best practice" can imply, however, that a single set of particular practices is optimal for every school, regardless of the community, the challenges, cultural and linguistic differences, or learners' biographies. We also know that the most effective teachers adapt, adjust, and modify instruction in response to particular students' strengths and needs. A teaching method or procedure cannot be transferred from one classroom to another without thoughtful and intentional adaptation. Approaches that claim to "standardize" teaching and learning will over-constrain generative teaching/learning.

Adaptive Action Builds Coherence

The bottom line is that generative teaching/learning is about using Adaptive Action to enact what is true and useful at a particular moment, in a particular context, with an eye toward the patterns that we want to see across the system. As teachers and learners in the system, we are agents with power to influence this complex and emergent reality— not cogs in a machine or pawns on a game board. Mandates will come and go, and we will respond to these mandates over time in ways that make sense to us. Our responses may be for better or worse. No mandate, regardless of how well-intentioned or how research-based it might be, will be implemented faithfully in the same way in every case. And no mandate can absolutely promise a direct increase in student achievement. There are too many unpredictable variables between the policy-maker and the student. Standardization is an impossible dream in a complex adaptive system.

Of course, we can understand that policy makers and high-level administrators feel the need to exert control over this huge system. Clearly, well-meaning leaders feel responsible for student achievement. They want to ensure that students are treated more or less equitably, no matter where they attend school. They want to make sure that all students have access to excellent instruction. They want to make sure that all teachers receive the professional development they need to support student achievement. The larger and more unwieldy the system, (logic would tell us) the more we need mechanisms like standards and high stakes accountability to ensure high achievement.

But those who understand complex adaptive systems take a different view. They know that everyone throughout a vibrant and sustainable system must have the freedom to adapt in response to feedback. Given that freedom, the system (and individuals within the system) will seek coherence because coherent patterns reduce tension in the system. Leaders have the responsibility to set conditions to constrain the system just enough (more fully discussed in Chapters 3 and 4) so that individuals can move to reduce that tension. Because "true and useful" patterns signal coherence in the system, we can use Adaptive Action to move toward "true and useful" practice.

Simple Rules Build Coherence

In addition to Adaptive Action, a short list of generative simple rules can set conditions for coherence. As we discussed in previous chapters, simple rules shape system patterns. If those rules support generative teaching/learning, the resulting patterns will help the system move in a coherent and sustainable direction. Explicit simple rules that help individuals shape those coherent patterns will be much more effective in the long run than lists of standards, tests, and high stakes accountability schemes. So we argue that educational policy makers and administrators will achieve coherence across the larger system if they focus on setting conditions for that coherence rather than issuing narrow mandates and implementing punitive accountability schemes.

This whole book argues for a particular list of simple rules that will support individuals and groups within a large educational system as they teach and learn. All seven rules contribute to a generative coherence across the system, but this chapter focuses on the need for teachers and

136

learners to search for the true and the useful. Again, we are reminded that generative teaching/learning is not about one individual at a time. It's about individuals within systems within larger systems.

The Architectural Model Builds Coherence

Architects have long known that "form follows function." Before they design a building, they gather information and think carefully about how that building will be used. They want to make sure that the design of the building aligns with its function. In her work as a school administrator, Royce borrowed that architectural rule as a metaphor for the design of organizational structures. In generative systems, form also follows function. That's simply another view of coherence. The structure or form of a system works best if it is coherent with its function.

In the Architectural Model, we focus on three interdependent questions: What are our shared beliefs? What are the primary functions of our system to support these beliefs? and What are the structures that will help us accomplish these functions and realize these beliefs? See Figure 6.5.

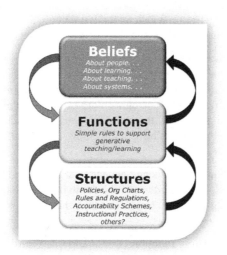

Figure 6.5: Architectural Model. System agents can use this model/method to check for coherence among their beliefs, system functions (simple rules) and structures.

HSD practitioners find this model particularly useful as they work together toward coherence or "fit" between what they say and what they actually do. Sometimes they work from the top of the model toward the bottom:

- What are our shared beliefs?
- What functions or simple rules help us live out those shared beliefs?
- What structures or practices will support those functions or simple rules?

Or sometimes they work from the bottom of the model up:

- What are our current structures or practices?
- How do those structures or practices force us to behave with each other? In other words, what do they say about what our current simple rules must be?
- What beliefs do those simple rules imply? Are those simple rules consistent with what we say we believe?

Here's an example that is familiar to educators everywhere. It has to do with how we use time in schools. Let's begin at the bottom of the model— and consider the time structures we see in schools today.

Structure: The school year has 175 to 185 days. Every student is expected to master at least 70% of the curricular standards at one grade within that period of time. At the end of that time, students who have mastered that percentage of the curriculum move to the next grade level. Students who do not exhibit that mastery repeat the grade level for another 175-185 days, regardless of how much below that 70% mark they have learned.

Function: Students and educators standardize the amount of time spent at a grade level, regardless of the depth or breadth of an individual students' learning. They are forced to function as timekeepers and measurers of standards.

Beliefs: These functions would appear to flow from the following beliefs:

- Time in a grade level is more important than evidence of learning.
- Standardization and efficiency are more important than response to individual differences.

One way to interpret this analysis is that students and staff are operating in a structure that forces them to function as timekeepers. They track the number of days left in a school year and each students' attendance record. The belief that is coherent with this structure and function is that "Time spent in class is more important than what a student learns." No educator really believes that, but the structures we have inherited, the structures that seem to help the bureaucracy work efficiently, would suggest that is precisely what we believe. Even a superficial consideration of other school structures would reveal similar inconsistencies between what we say we believe and how we use our structures to function.

Here are some reminders that HSD practitioners have found helpful in using this model/method:

- Using this model does not call for extended word-smithing of lofty statements about values and beliefs. In our experience, such statements can take a great deal of time and ultimately may serve little real purpose. It's just about getting clear about basic beliefs or assumptions, relative to the work we have to do. What do we consider true, useful, and important about how we treat people and about how we get our work done?

- Belief statements are only valuable if they lead to action. We need to move our conversations to action. Simple rules are a powerful way to connect our beliefs to the structures we need to build, sustain, or abandon.

- A functioning system is made up of different types of structures that work interdependently: policies; regulations; procedures; communication channels; resource exchanges; decision-making processes; evaluation and accountability schemes; instructional practices, and professional development practices.

- The Architectural Model is both a model and a method. As a model, it can help us understand the coherence among beliefs, functions, and structures. As a method, it can help us generate options for action, both in our individual and our collective work.

The Architectural Model can be used in many ways—as support for long-range planning for the whole district or as a frame for a conversation about literacy instruction at a single grade level. Here is a story one principal tells about how he and his staff used it:

> I am fairly new to this school, and when I arrived, I realized that we have a school where the population of children has changed over time. We are now serving more students from poverty, and we have more English learners each year. But most of our teachers have been

*here for a long time, and they had not really talked
openly about these changes. I knew that we needed to
understand our students better, and that we had some
work to do on our equity piece. For our first step in that
direction, we used the Architectural Model. Two of the
teachers planned and led the meeting. It was wonderful
because they really did the work, ran it by me, and I
said go for it. Because I felt like they have been at this
school a long time; they're invested in this school.
Questions coming out of their mouths are much more
important than from mine. I didn't want the other
teachers to think this was an agenda from the outside.
So it was a beautiful day. I was in the back of the room.
They had the conversation all set up with Architectural
Model, asking the teachers about their beliefs, simple
rules, and the structures related to equity for all our
students. The conversation—it was like picture perfect,
just exactly how you would want a long conversation
about equity to start. Afterward, both of those teachers
just kept saying this model really helped us get to the
conversations we needed.*

—Elementary Principal

In this book, we argue that our goal in schools should be generative teaching/learning, which refers to the meanings agents make and the actions they take to adapt toward coherence across the whole, part, or greater whole. We are convinced that this stance toward teaching and learning will encourage everyone to use Adaptive Action and will increase the potential for adaptive capacity across the system, at all scales. If that is our belief, we should be able to apply the Architectural Model to check for coherence as we carry out our functions (or simple rules) and as we develop options for action. Table 6.1 is a working document that shows how we are working toward an articulation of beliefs, functions and structures coherent with generative teaching/learning.

Table 6.1: Architectural Model applied to generative /learning

Beliefs	**Generative learners...** • assume that the world is full of complex, adaptive systems/networks • take an inquiry stance, seeking patterns that make sense • work together to solve problems, giving and granting voice to others • use multiple ways (language, nonverbal signs, technology, etc.) to make sense of the world • are able to use their background knowledge to make sense of the world. • take risks to try challenging tasks **Generative school transformation . . .** • happens when Generative Learning is central to everyone in the system——across and up/down (see bullets above for beliefs about learning) • everyone works toward shared meanings (goals, models, methods, etc.)
Functions	• Teach and learn in every interaction. • Attend to the whole, the part, and the greater whole. • See, understand, and influence patterns. • Recognize and build on assets of self and others. • Look for the true and the useful. • Act with courage. • Seek joy in learning
Structures	• Adaptive Action (journals, stories, debriefing, plans) • HSD Methods and Models • Generative instructional practices • Professional learning communities • Classroom walk-throughs • Newsletters and blogs • Statements of mission, vision, goals • Performances/presentations • Conferences with students, staff, parents, and other stakeholders • Procedures • Performance expectations • Accountability systems for student achievement

NOW WHAT? BUILD COHERENCE FOR ADAPTIVE CAPACITY

As human systems dynamics practitioners, we continually try to see, understand, and take action to support true and useful patterns. This focus on true and useful knowledge contributes to the emerging patterns in our thinking/actions—which we have labeled "patterns of praxis." In our praxis, we integrate theory and practice. Whatever the focus of our work, we can contribute to the health and sustainability of our systems if we focus on both the true and the useful.

When this insistence on the true and the useful becomes a part of the culture in a classroom, on a campus, or throughout the district, the system will shift. One HSD practitioner put it this way:

> . . . the change in the way people in the district think and interact has been pretty dramatic . . . . I think that there's a lot more focus on what we're doing, how we're doing it and what impact it's having. So everybody's talking about "patterns." And talking about "the difference that makes a difference" and what's "true and useful." And I think initially, it probably felt a little bit staged, but I think it becomes real the more you use it and the more various people understand it and embrace it. . . . . .

> —*Central Office Administrator*

NOW WHAT? USE THESE RESOURCES TO LEARN MORE

Burns, D. (2007). *Systemic action research: A strategy for whole system change.* Bristol, UK: Policy Press.

Eoyang, G. H. and Holladay, R. (2013). *Adaptive action: Leveraging change in your organization.* Palo Alton, CA: Stanford University Press.

Fullan, M. (2011). *Change leader: Learning to do what matters most.* San Francisco, Jossye-Bass.

Patterson, L., Baldwin, S., Araujo, J., Shearer, R., & Stewart, M. A. (2010). Look, think, act: Using action research to sustain reform in complex teaching/learning ecologies, *Journal of Inquiry and Action in Education, 3*, 3, 139-157. https://journal.buffalostate.edu/index.php/soe/index

National Center for Literacy Education (NCLE), Literacy in Learning Exchange. http://www.literacyinlearningexchange.org/

Schmoker, M. J. (2011). *Focus: Elevating the essentials to radically improve student learning.* Alexandria, VA: Association for the Supervision and Curriculum Development.

CHAPTER 7:
Courage

The HSD approach to school transformation is radical. It is radical in two senses of that word. First, it addresses the "root" or the underlying dynamics of teaching and learning in human organizations. Second, it sometimes requires extreme actions——actions that are not typical or particularly comfortable in a bureaucracy. Typically, educators are not prone to risky decisions, but dealing with the uncertainty and inevitable change within complex adaptive systems requires risk-taking. This chapter focuses on why risk-taking is critical to generative teaching/learning.

Central Challenge	Encourage risk-taking
Simple Rule	Act with courage.
Concepts, Methods, and Models	Three Kinds of Change
Guiding Questions	What does courage have to do with tension and unpredictability? What are the three kinds of change in complex systems? So what about courage and risk-taking in schools? Now what? Act with courage to build adaptive capacity. Now what? Use these resources to learn more.

Learners must take risks. They cannot be certain whether they will succeed. Sometimes they can't even be sure how to take the next step. And that is how we must move forward in complex adaptive systems. It takes curiosity to encourage us to take the first step into uncertainty and it takes courage to move forward into the unknown. Here is how one principal sees herself as a risk-taker:

> I admit to being a perfectionist—the most organized person, the one that almost always has the answer or knows how to get the answer. Thinking ahead ten steps in every which way. So I've definitely modeled that, and I see that replicated in all of my teachers. They want to be the absolute best teachers in the district. But I've never been public about my struggles. And I think that comes along with my position as campus principal—my assumption that I've got to be a certain way, and you're never going to see me sweat. If I make mistakes, I will definitely own up to it and apologize, but people never want a leader to constantly make mistakes and then be looked at as incompetent. So I think that trying to find that middle ground now for me, and that's been a task in itself. I think I set up this pattern for my teachers. I think they are so focused on being the best because I set it up for them. So my goal now is to share more of my struggles. I'm trying to create that balance where I'm not looking incompetent because that's not what I want either. But I've come to realize that I need to be vocal about my challenges, about how I struggled through them, and how I helped to resolve them.

> —Elementary School Principal

Like this principal, we want to appear competent and confident in our decisions. When our colleagues come to us for help, we want to have the right answer. And we want to be sure of it. By now, however, it should be clear that, from a human systems dynamics perspective, we see that our worlds are neither certain nor predictable.

As we pointed out at the beginning of this book, the field of human systems dynamics examines how humans live, work, and play together in these complex and unpredictable systems. In this chapter, we focus on a simple rule that helps us deal with this unsettling unpredictability:

Act with courage.

This simple rule encourages us to stand in inquiry as we reach out to set conditions for more appropriate patterns, even when we meet opposition and when the new patterns seem risky. More importantly, this chapter explains why uncertainty is natural and essential in a complex adaptive system.

WHAT DOES COURAGE HAVE TO DO WITH TENSION AND UNPREDICTABILITY?

Complex adaptive systems are open to influence, information, and energy from their environments. (Remember that these environments are simply larger systems of which the smaller ones are a part). That openness is problematic for those of us who want neat and tidy tasks and happily-ever-after endings. But one reality of complex systems is that, as these new influences enter the system, the dynamics become less and less predictable. Researchers say that open systems are "indeterminate." There is no particular goal toward which a system moves. There is no master narrative that can tell us what to expect. These new influences coming into the system introduce multiple diversities; tension builds in these differences; and the system self-organizes or shifts to relieve that building tension.

We can think of tension as a build-up of energy in the system, energy around whatever differences bring stress to the system. Friction is an indication of this tension in physical systems and can serve as a metaphor to help us understand it in human systems. Friction is essential to a machine, in that it slows the movement of one part against the other. Without some amount of friction, the parts would slide around and not get traction to do their work. Friction becomes dysfunctional, however, when energy builds to the point that the parts cannot move. In a mechanical system, we need to find and sustain an optimal level of friction. Complex adaptive systems are not machines, but the concept of mechanical friction gives us a sense of how tension functions in a CAS.

As we explained in Chapter 3, tension emerges at points of difference at any scale in the system, and self-organization in the system results from the actions individuals and groups take to resolve those tensions. The following are some examples of difference that generate tension.

- Tension between ourselves and others emerges from our individual uniqueness, the multiple, unpredictable ways we are different from each other. Sometimes those differences are fun and exciting——bringing the tension of new love or friendship in the excitement and mystery of getting to know someone new.

At other times those differences can be frustrating or frightening. When I don't understand who you are or what you bring, or when I don't know what to expect from you, I might feel out of control or afraid.

- Tension emerges when we experience the difference between where we are and where we want to be. It is our ability to imagine what life can be like or to remember what it was like that creates the emotional tension that propels us toward action to move toward what we want or away from what we don't want. Similarly, we experience tension in the difference between what we have and what we want, and between what I know and what I don't know.

- We experience tension as we observe differences between and among others. Our imaginations and memories are triggered as we observe tension in others, and we take action to intervene, to join in, or to damp the differences we see. When we see bullying or cruelty, we are generally moved to take action; when we see joy and friendship, it's likely that we will want to move toward that.

Any of these examples reflect how the tension in our lives emerges as we take action to find the appropriate level of coherence across the many differences in our lives. The trick is to recognize these tensions, to embrace them, and to stand in inquiry as we set conditions for self-organizing learning for ourselves and for others.

These stories of two principals reveal how tension emerges on their campuses:

> *And then our staff decided to focus on shared reading——that's where we need to learn together to help **all** the students. But it has been a shift, definitely, and shifts cause tension. Last year, I don't think I had a staff meeting that was unpleasant all year. . . . People were pretty happy . . . but there was no urgency. This year, the last two staff meetings have been tough. . . . But I think that's probably a good sign, because I think when you grow and change, it's uncomfortable sometimes.*

> *—Elementary School Principal*

> *So I've really been pushing the teachers on our staff to share their process. They do these cycles of inquiry when they have something they're struggling with. We do it all the time. For example, this student's struggling with a*

particular skill or concept, or the whole class is struggling.
How can we help them? We try something, it works or
doesn't. We reflect. We go back and we try some more.
And then, when we have some results, we share them. But
we don't often share the messy process that we went
through to get to those results. So I've noticed someone
will say, "Oh well, I don't do that; I do this and I found it's
very effective." And it makes others either get defensive or
feel bad. So I've been asking people to explain, "Well, how
did you get to that point? What was your original
question? What did you try that didn't work?" So other
teachers can see that there's a whole process of getting
there. It's not magic.

—*Elementary School Principal*

We welcome tension (in all these senses) because it triggers self-organization, learning, or transformation—all terms for how complex adaptive systems respond to tension, incoherence, and uncertainty. We want to emphasize that we are not victims of these tensions in the system. As human beings, we are agents in the system, not passive components. We are subjects who act; not objects to be acted upon. We have the capacity to take action, and our actions can set conditions that influence how the system will self-organize. That leads us to back to the simple rule that is the focus of this chapter: **Act with courage**. Below, we offer concrete suggestions for how teachers and learners in schools can do just that.

Time Out for Reflection

Think about your system and the daily tensions that build up from differences bumping against one another. What are the differences that generate tension in your system? Think of four to five such differences. Imagine how those tensions have triggered change across the system. (The change might be either 'good' or 'bad' for the system.) Tell a story about how that has happened recently in your system.

WHAT ARE THE THREE KINDS OF CHANGE IN COMPLEX SYSTEMS?

Effective change in human organizations depends on whether change agents can (and will) see, understand, and influence patterns so that the system can function in adaptive and self-sustaining ways. In other words, if we want to transform schools, we need to imagine what patterns of behavior in classrooms, faculty meetings, and boardrooms are the most adaptive and sustainable over the long term. We need to hypothesize about the CDE (Chapter 4)—the conditions for generative teaching/learning in that context. In other words, we need to recognize the expectations, structures, and routines (constraints) that might best help students, teachers, administrators, parents, and community members work together, learn from one another, and make decisions about how to adapt to their inevitable challenges. That requires us to embrace uncertainty as we admit we cannot predict or control the future. It requires us to be courageous enough to set conditions for the patterns we want to see; and then curious enough to relax and watch with interest as the system dynamics do their work. To do that, it helps us to understand the nature of change, particularly the three kinds of change: simple; dynamic; and dynamical. Table 7.1 provides a brief overview of the explanations that follow.

Table 7.1: Three kinds of change. This table briefly outlines the differences between the types of change we see in systems.

SIMPLE CHANGE	DYNAMIC CHANGE	DYNAMICAL CHANGE
An external force causes a shift from one stable position to a different, equally stable position	Forces that act on a system can be known and measured, making change predictable and measurable.	Multiple forces acting on a system are unknown and unknowable, and massively entangled.
We think only of before and after, with no consideration for what happens during the shift.	We think of the measurable and predictable arch or stages of change.	We function best by seeing, understanding, and influencing the system to adapt toward fitness.
Describes change in a system that is closed, low dimension, linear.	Describes change in a system that is closed, low dimension, linear	Describes change in a system that is open, high dimension, and nonlinear.

Simple Change

Simple change points to the kind of change that is most familiar and easiest to understand. It means something moves (or is moved) from one place to another. (Physicists call this "static" change, but we think "simple" makes more sense for our purposes.) Here's an example: A soccer ball sits on a field. Someone picks up the ball and moves it to another spot. It's in one place, then it's in another place, with no consideration of what happened to it in the meantime. That is what we mean by simple change.

Simple change begins and ends with an object at rest. Simple change occurs when a force moves that object to a different, equally stable, position. Simple change is highly predictable, controllable, and easily measured. Once you decide to move something, you do it and you know whether or not you have finished, and you can judge how well you accomplished the move by measuring against the original plan.

One way to think about simple change in human systems is the children's game "musical chairs," at the beginning of the game, before the chairs are moved. The music begins, and the children walk in a circle. The music stops, and everyone finds a chair. When the number of chairs is equal to the number of children, and everyone sits down, this is a simple change—children standing up; children sitting down. It is highly predictable—music, walk, sit, music, walk, and sit. It is very controllable—turn the music on; turn it off. And it's easily measured—did everyone start, then stop, then find a chair? But for most children that "game" would quickly become boring; there's not enough tension in the system to sustain interest. The fun comes as we introduce a bit of turbulence and unpredictability. Remove a chair before each round of music (or shift the conditions), and we have a different kind of change!

To accomplish simple change, we just have to answer two questions: which direction will the system move? How do I get it to move? Or, in a school, we might say, "Where do we want to be? What will it take to get there?"

This perspective shows up when we believe that "tweaking" the system will bring about change. We think simple change can be useful when used within a larger, over-arching design for change. The problem comes when we try to use simple change by itself, without considering what underlying conditions (the CDE) are being shifted. When the complexity of the system is ignored, an intentional change may just disrupt the system. For example, a principal of a middle school might:

- Change the teachers' room assignments, putting all the math teachers together; all the social studies teachers together with no follow-up to help them develop collaborative relationships.

- Train teachers and students about fire and tornado drill procedures.

- Publish test data for one year with no explanation, interpretation, or information about the context.
- Schedule time for teachers to meet in Professional Learning Communities, but offer no support for how to set conditions for that kind of professional learning.

The year Royce was going into ninth grade, her district opened a new school building. It was built on an open space concept, with acres of carpeted space and movable walls that could shift to allow for multiple instructional arrangements. It was a lovely facility, but the teachers were given no real training in how to take advantage of this kind of flexibility. Within a month of starting school, the portable walls had been erected as permanent and each teacher was teaching accordingly. The best way to think about those changes is that they are simple: teachers were apart; now they are together. Students were in the classroom; now they are not. Test data was in the report from the state; now it's in the newspaper. There was no time for teachers to meet; now they meet weekly. Each change is highly predictable—by the person who is creating the move. Each change is controllable—by the person who is in power. Each change is easily measured—it either happened or it did not. That does not mean that each change contributes to the desired ends, or that it sets the conditions for self-organizing dynamics.

- Locating teachers geographically together won't work unless they are also given time and skills and unless they have the will to work together toward a commonly shared goal.
- Publishing standards won't change how children learn, unless instruction and instructional support systems change.
- Conducting high stakes testing won't change how children learn, unless the data are used to inform strategies at all levels of the system and sufficient resources are made available.
- Giving professionals 45 minutes a week for collaborative learning makes no difference until they are asking questions and have new sources of information to help them consider alternative approaches.

Simple change is effective when we deal with simple, linear processes that have explicit, unambiguous objectives and predictable outcomes. In other words, simple change is most appropriate with issues in the highly organized corner of the Landscape Diagram (See Chapter 3). Managerial functions like taking inventory or keeping attendance records are examples. Very few processes in school systems, however, fit this description. Simple change does not—it cannot—allow us to consider multiple, interdependent agents or factors in the system. It doesn't consider the myriad differences that exist in human systems. It simply will not bring about the whole system change that's needed to help us meet our current challenges in schools.

At the national scale, the education system is a complex maze of interdependence and multiple causality. The challenges are neither simple nor linear, and reforms involving simple change will inevitably disappoint. Some people say these simple solutions are like teaching a pig to sing: It frustrates you and irritates the pig. Typical school reform initiatives assume that simple change is effective. In other words, many reformers seem to assume that once they make a policy change, things will "stay put." The attempts at comprehensive school reform in the mid-1980s, in the wake of *Nation at Risk*, could be read as a series of policy changes based on the assumption that simple change would trigger improvement. Student achievement is low?—Introduce standards. Standards alone don't help?—Mandate standardized tests. Tests don't do the trick?—Introduce high stakes and accountability schemes. Still no significant movement in student achievement? –Develop new, higher standards. Now develop a new test to fit the new standards. And so on. Apparently, we have assumed that each simple policy change would lead in a predictable way to higher student achievement. And when those clear results didn't happen, we introduced a new or stronger simple change.

If we believe today's headlines, it would seem that these major reforms have been inconsequential in terms of clear results. Headlines seem to say that—even after thirty years of major reforms—we are still a nation at risk. Of course, that's not true. These policy moves have dramatically influenced instructional practice and student learning. We have seen both intended and unintended consequences. But we continue to hear urgent calls to address the student achievement crisis in schools. Educators know that "things have changed," but this sequence of simple changes has not significantly shifted the underlying dynamics that prompted the initial concerns. These reforms have not set conditions for school systems to adapt in response to the urgent demands of ever-changing economic, political and cultural environments.

In terms of the simple rule that is the focus of this chapter, reformers who advocate simple change solutions want to control the outcomes; they are simply not willing to embrace the uncertainty inherent in self-organizing systems.

Dynamic Change

The second kind of change in complex adaptive systems is **dynamic change**. Dynamic change suggests the movement of an object or process along a smooth path from its starting point to a logical destination. Throwing a ball from first base to home plate is a concrete example of dynamic energy. Remember the soccer ball from the example of simple change? Skilled soccer players know how to see the distance from the ball to the goal; they consider the wind and other forces that act on the ball in its flight; and they judge the arc and power to use in kicking the ball. That is an example of dynamic change.

We sometimes also think of organic processes as manifesting dynamic change when we think of the steps in a predictable sequence. For example, the life cycle of a butterfly often serves as a metaphor for the dynamic unfolding of these discrete steps. First the egg hatches into a caterpillar, which eats leaves until it builds a cocoon, from which it eventually emerges as a lovely butterfly. Human development, by the way, is often thought of as dynamic change—gradual and continual change from one distinct stage to the next distinct and predictable stage and to the next. Think of Piaget's stages of cognitive development and Kohlberg's stages of moral development. Or think of a leader who sees his or her role as the trigger of a chain reaction that, once started, will progress according to several pre-determined and predictable stages toward the identified objective. In all those examples, we see the characteristics of dynamic change, and it is useful to focus on that gradual and predictable change. When we look more closely at those changes, however, we see that human development is not precisely the same for every person. We can neither predict nor control human development according to what we know from Piaget or Kohlberg, but we can get a sense of the progression—the general pattern of change.

To predict and control change processes that are truly dynamic, we must answer two questions: What are the initial conditions? and What are the forces working on the object? If we have these two kinds of data, we can make decisions about how to facilitate or support the process toward its predictable conclusion. As with simple perspectives on change, dynamic change works wonderfully—when the system is appropriately constrained.

The school leader who engages in dynamic change sees her role as 1) learning as much as possible about what is happening, 2) knowing what is likely to happen next, and 3) knowing just what steps will generate the forces needed to move the system along that predictable path. Data are critical—data to inform participants about where the system starts, where it is in the expected sequence of steps or stages, and where it is headed. Of course, the leader would be expected to offer appropriate support at each step in the process and to recognize when the system is transitioning from one stage to the next:

- Set objectives and outcomes (assuming that teachers and students will move smoothly toward those endpoints).

- Identify and address one or more root causes of the problem.

- Hypothesize about strategies to address those causes.

- Track trends of change over time.

- Expect developmental phases during an implementation process (like storming, forming, norming, and performing).

- Assume all students progress through learning at similar rates and according to similar patterns.

Like simple change, dynamic change is most appropriate for decisions and issues that are less complex and more knowable. The more valid and reliable data we have the more predictable the path of development should be. Or at least that is what many reformers assume:

- Grade-level standards and frequent benchmark tests for student performance are useful because they point to the gradually increasing knowledge and skills expected at each level.

- Because teaching contributes directly to increases in student learning, teacher evaluations should be linked to student performance.

- The insistence on "evidence-based" programs shows confidence in the scientific process to identify programs that achieve targeted results, regardless of environmental conditions.

- Accountability schemes that make test scores public are intended to provide information to parents and businesses in the belief that they will pressure administrators and teachers to improve student performance.

To be more specific, the 2002 federal legislation, *No Child Left Behind (NCLB)*, was based on the assumption that school improvement is essentially a dynamic change. At first that legislation was lauded as a bipartisan attempt to raise math and reading achievement across the country and to close the infamous achievement gap. Even the language — "leave no child behind"—assumes a linear journey from one place to another. The law's centerpiece was the requirement to hold states accountable for setting curriculum standards and for measuring student achievement as "adequate yearly progress." Adequate yearly progress

(AYP) was the attempt to quantify dynamic progress in student achievement and to hold schools accountable for dynamic improvement over a predetermined period of time. Many critics point to AYP as the most problematic aspect of NCLB. President Obama's "Blueprint" for reauthorization of that legislation also makes the basic assumption of a smooth and predictable journey of transition, as does his *Race to the Top* competitive funding program.

Strategies based on a dynamic perspective on change can work if system constraints are a fit. They work best when we have valid knowledge about how a particular process works and when we have accurate data about what the system is doing (which is seldom the case in schools). They work when these processes are allowed to act independently to bring the system toward a desired end (without undue or unpredicted influences). They work effectively when no opposing forces are at work in the system. When conditions are right, a dynamic perspective on change works beautifully—mostly they work in non-human mechanistic systems, like launching the Space shuttle and bringing it home.

Strategies like AYP are problematic, however, because they assume that teaching and learning are essentially dynamic processes. They treat teaching and learning processes as though they are predictable and controllable, working together to progress according to a smooth trajectory, moving toward a pre-determined end, and supported by complete and accurate information. The central difficulty with this assumption is that children's development and human learning are not predictable. We cannot predict how each student (or adult) in our schools will respond. Even the most complicated set of standards cannot account for variations among individuals. Even the most sophisticated accountability system (or the latest statistical procedure) cannot completely account for the nonlinear interactions between and among agents in schools. Human learning and growth are complex adaptive processes.

Yet another challenge to this dynamic approach is that it assumes perfect and complete knowledge, which is not possible in the realm of public education. Education is not a closed system. It is part of greater social, economic, political, and cultural systems, and the boundaries among them all are permeable. Districts and campuses are influenced by changing demographics, diverse community expectations, and political pressures. Human communities are complex adaptive systems—the whole, the part, and the greater whole. It is impossible to have perfect and complete knowledge of the things that influence teaching and learning in the real world.

When conditions are as complex as these—when diversity abounds; when agents are free to make unanticipated choices; when each action has the potential to influence every other action; and when things are changing quickly—a dynamic perspective can actually be a barrier to sustainable change in the system. In such a system, dynamic approaches provide too much constraint for the system to self-organize. For example, relying on carrots and sticks as incentives for learning introduce constraints into the system that can actually inhibit the kind of creative and critical problem solving they were intended to support. Although we can use the language of dynamic change to help us talk about strategies for school improvement, we can't assume that all groups or individuals will move along the targeted path in a uniform way. It is problematic to assume that dynamic change is the only force—or even the major force—at work in schools.

Dynamical (Self-Organizing/Emergent/Generative) Change

"Dynamical" is a word physicists and mathematicians use for change that is unpredictable, but not random. **Dynamical change** is what happens when a complex system self-organizes. It is the kind of change we have been describing throughout this book—unpredictable, nonlinear, surprising, and adaptive. The system may look as if nothing is changing, but all of a sudden there's a breakthrough. Breakthroughs can be all sizes, and each one contributes to the transformation of the whole.

Think about an avalanche. As snow piles up on the mountainside, the crystals of ice press down on each other, and tension builds in the system. It continues to build until the system can no longer contain it and the system shifts. Now if you look at that mountainside from the distance or at shorter intervals, it looks as though nothing is happening. But when you observe up close, you can see the smaller shifts that relieve tension across the whole. Limited amounts of snow shift and re-settle in small avalanches in isolated areas across the mountain. Over time, as more snow continues to fall, the tension builds until even the slightest stressor--wind, air vibrations of loud noises, one too many snowflakes--will cause a major shift, and an entire side of the mountain can be engulfed in a major avalanche.

We see dynamical change in human systems as well—in family relationships, in friendships, and in teaching/learning experiences inside and outside schools. Teachers establish norms and routines as constraints that may shape the learning, but they can't control it. Each individual student has agency—and the option not to comply. An experienced teacher might be able to describe generally how a child will respond to a hypothetical situation, but there is no way to predict exact responses to a particular stimulus at a particular place and time.

From the HSD perspective, generative learning is a specific case of dynamical change. Each student, teacher, administrator, parent, and staff member brings his or her unique and changing needs, perspectives, expectations, and aspirations into the system at a particular time and place. At the campus, district, and policy scales, agents come together with the potential for self-organization and adaptive change. Their curiosity, embrace of uncertainty, and courage help set the conditions for shared agreements and adaptive action in response to challenges inside and outside the system.

In systems where dynamical change is in motion, the role of the leader is to

- Set conditions that influence the system's self-organizing process;
- Watch for patterns across the system;
- Understand those patterns; and
- Take action that can gradually influence the path the system might take to generate patterns of adaptability and productivity.

The role of the leader is to anticipate patterns that may emerge rather than to predict particular results. It's about setting conditions to influence the path of the system, rather than controlling it. As we have said in previous chapters (especially Chapter 4), it's about seeing, understanding, and influencing patterns in systems at all levels.

> **Time Out for Reflection**
>
> *Many of our decisions in schools are informed by data, and the ways we use data are influenced by whether we are looking for simple, dynamic, or dynamical change. For example, there is a significant difference in using a single data point to inform our decisions, looking for trends in the data over time, or focusing on patterns of stability and surprise. Think about times when you and your colleagues used a single data point (example: the 3rd graders' math scores last year) to inform your decisions. Were you assuming that, if you did a particular thing you could make the math scores go up? That would be simple change. How would we look at data differently if we assumed the data came from dynamic or dynamical change? Would we need multiple data sources? Would we need to look at changes over time? How would that look in your system? How would that influence your options for action?*

The challenge is to know when to expect (and support) dynamical change. Here are some suggestions. When you see one or more of these kinds of patterns, be aware of them as signals of nonlinear and dynamical change.

- **Fractal patterns**—when change at one level mirrors, instigates, or prevents change at another level. A new superintendent or a significant change in the school board triggers change throughout the system in the same way that significant changes at one school can have an impact on what happens at another school.

- **A tipping point**—when a system is poised far from equilibrium, a small change can trigger an avalanche. A system can withstand a number of small changes or challenges and continue to move forward incrementally or not appear to move at all. At some point, however, those changes build so much pressure or tension, that the system "explodes" — often resulting in big unintended and unanticipated changes for good or ill.

- **Intermittent jumps and cascades**—when the system seems "stuck" as tension accumulates then breaks loose with abandon, bringing about unexpected and unpredictable results. No system has a single tipping-point collapse and then is finished with a change. In its attempt to find equilibrium, a system is constantly holding and building tension until it cannot manage it, releasing that tension through any number of ways. Superintendents resign and leave in short order over an event that doesn't seem so important to others. Parents who have been quiet over time, suddenly show up in large numbers at a school board meeting to air their concerns. Teachers get their fill of students' lackadaisical attitudes and take drastic action. When such a surprising event occurs, you can expect other jumps, perhaps in distant parts of the system.

- **Networks of connections** —when links form across the system that can either hold it stable or move it quickly into new patterns. Parent-teacher associations across a district can contribute to stability and growth in a district; they can also be a network for spreading rumors and questions about district policy.

- **Resonance of self-organizing patterns**—when interacting parts generate coherent system-wide patterns. This is how culture emerges in a group or system. People interact in ways that generate patterns that exert influence across the system. Soon, others begin to interact according to those patterns, creating a system-wide pattern of behavior or expectation. For example, in the mid- to latter part of the 20th century, no one thought much about learning standards that were different from state to state, town to town, or even school to school. When people began to think about it, however, the creation of common standards became a pattern across the country as more people heard and came to believe they had found the answer to school reform in standard requirements.

If we understand that dynamical change sets the conditions for generative learning, we know that our actions can influence the system in essentially unpredictable ways. But we also need to watch for patterns that emerge in classrooms and schools that signal the system's movement toward generative learning, and we need to look for ways to sustain and strengthen those generative patterns. When we understand the dynamics of complex, adaptive systems, we can trust the self-organizing process itself. We admit that we were never in "control" anyway, that our best path is to stand in inquiry and be ready to adapt as needed. That knowledge can give us courage.

SO WHAT ABOUT COURAGE AND RISK-TAKING IN SCHOOLS?

What do the Landscape Diagram and these three perspectives on change mean for those of us who want to transform schools? It simply means that deep change in schools is risky business. One of the stickiest issues facing school leaders is that people in schools have been socialized to think that there is an easy path, that there are silver bullets for our instructional challenges. Of course, the most recent wave of reform doesn't speak of "silver bullets," but of "best practice" and "fidelity of implementation" of "evidence-based practice." We have come to expect clear and easy solutions. We tend to avoid the risks inherent in radical change.

We also expect our leaders to be decisive and confident as they tell us which best practice to use. We tend to distrust leaders who are more tentative about what will work with students. Students also distrust teachers who are tentative about their instructional decisions, as this teacher explains,

> *Well, I get very honest with my kids. I tell them that my job is to not tell you what the answer is. My job is to help you think and to help you formulate your own analysis and your own questions. You're probably going to be frustrated with me, and you're going to have to decide what's important to you. You're going to have to decide*

the solutions and what evidence you're going to use to support your claims. And often, there's a tremendous amount of frustration. I've actually had kids tell me, "Well, you just don't know how to teach." And so I ask them, "What do you mean by that?" And they'll just say, "Well, you're supposed to be up there and tell me what I need to write down."

—Secondary School Teacher

This same frustration plagues all of us who hunger for simple change and live every day in the realm of dynamical change for learners and the people and institutions that support them.

Three Kinds of Change and Generative Teaching/Learning

The previous sections of this chapter lay the conceptual groundwork for leaders and teachers who want to break away from the traditional expectations of school reform and make more mindful and generative decisions. As we explained in Chapter 2, the Learning Landscape, we can use an adaptation of the Landscape Diagram as a thinking tool to interpret the patterns we see among students and our colleagues. When the system is tightly constrained (bottom left), learning may be seen as a process of internalizing familiar patterns. This might include memorizing the multiplication tables or the periodic table of elements. Teaching from a simple change perspective would be explicit and teacher-directed. Student knowledge might be measured by true/false, multiple-choice, or short answer formats.

With those tight constraints, we might also see learning as dynamic change, if we are focusing on the process rather than the beginning and the end result. In dynamic change, we would see a pattern of development over time, for example, increasing skill development assessed along a continuum. This might include psychomotor skill development or the development of fluency in reading and writing. It means assessing learning according to an externally derived set of standards that are sequential and developmental. It means students progressing through grade levels in lock-step progression that is measured by time rather than level of skill or understanding. As you can see, simple and dynamic approaches to teaching and learning are sometimes appropriate, depending on the learning objective. They are also the only ways we have had in the past for thinking about the organizational structures and activities that support teaching and learning.

But human systems dynamics offers us a new way to think about more open-ended teaching and learning. In contrast, when the system is less constrained, it may also be under-constrained as learners may not have the concepts or structures they need to move forward. This would happen when learners are seeking patterns in information that seems random. Although many learners enjoy the exploration and creativity required in this area of the learning landscape, if they remain in that experience too long, they may become confused or frustrated before disengaging altogether.

In the middle area of the landscape, the system is appropriately constrained for **dynamical change**. We think that this area of the Learning Landscape is similar to Vygotsky's zone of proximal development (1978), where learners can perform the new learning objective, but only with assistance or support. The assistance from the more knowledgeable other (a teacher, a parent, or a peer) provides appropriate constraint so that the new learning can emerge. As the learner becomes more proficient, fluent, and confident, the need for this support/constraint diminishes.

Although educators sometimes act as if they are dealing with simple or dynamic change, the changes they actually see in their classrooms and schools often more clearly fit descriptions of dynamical change. The systems are open to multiple and interdependent influences; they are diverse with a vengeance; and they are constantly moving and changing, with or without our intervention. That kind of learning environment calls for courage from both teachers and learners!

These descriptions clearly sound like our experiences with dynamical change in schools, and they remind us of the conflict that comes when we bump up against policies and procedures that assume simple or dynamical change. This is how one teacher described his experience with that conflict:

> On one hand, I grew up with this foundation of wonder
> and curiosity and "be what you want." But in schools,
> the need to control and create good workers and order, I
> think, overrode the desire to be free thinkers. So that
> created a conflict for me, you know? School was a piece
> of cake for me. I never was challenged. I don't remember
> working very hard in school, and I was an A student.
> There was a lot of "this is how it is, do this, do this" —
> until I had a teacher in 11th grade who really valued
> what we thought. And I was in a place where I got to
> design and build things. I designed and built this gazebo
> for a teacher in high school. I designed and built a sign

162

with electricity running into it, you know that's still in
front of my high school. And I got course credit for that.
That was when I started to make that shift away from
"this is what you need to know; this is what's
important," and a whole world started opening up.

—Secondary Teacher

When school transformation initiatives acknowledge the power of dynamical change, we will look for "coherence" rather than "standardization." Our criteria for evaluation will have more to do more with "appropriateness" than with "achieving pre-determined objectives." Our process for achieving this fit, both internally and externally, must allow for clear and thorough assessment, for multiple data sources, for thoughtful review and interpretation, and for subsequent action. As we discussed in Chapter 2, dynamical school transformation calls for generative teaching/learning and Adaptive Action—seeing, understanding, and influencing patterns by setting conditions that increase or decrease constraints on the system. In other words, school transformation calls for the courage to set conditions for dynamical change, and when we set conditions for dynamical change, we build adaptive capacity.

Time Out for Reflection
Think of your most perplexing challenge. Does that challenge involve dynamical change? Can you imagine how multiple Adaptive Action cycles might help you work through that challenge? How might that play out over time?

Clearly, this emergent or generative work is uncertain. The system needs some amount of this tension and uncertainty to move forward, but too much uncertainty can be dysfunctional. As agents in the system, our response to this uncertainty is critical. We need to be curious enough to engage in this unpredictable learning and courageous enough to take the cognitive and interpersonal risks that we may face. It's not hard to think of situations in schools that hold this kind of uncertainty.

Here are two—one about adult learning and one about students:

I've had some positive interactions with the union, which
were big issues and, knock on wood; we're on the same
road now. That was me taking a deep breath and
stepping out and saying "Hey, we can't function like this
again." Last year was not good, and it was important for
me to say, "we can't work like this so we need to figure

out common ground and know that we're both here for the same purpose."

—District Supervisor

I think some kids just want me to tell them what I want them to know. They might as well say, "Just tell me. I don't care how or why it's supposed to work but just give it to me. . . . Give me the answer." And they don't really care about the baby steps that get them there. They don't want to take the risk of asking a question or making a guess."

—Secondary Teacher

Setting Conditions for Risk-taking

How do we work in schools so that we are setting appropriate conditions for dynamical learning across this landscape? How do we set conditions for more organized work when appropriate? How do we know when it's time to give learners (both children and adults) more freedom, to encourage them to move toward the creative zone? How can individuals or groups hope to understand and/or influence the systems around them unless they can know how to navigate the Learner's Landscape? These are the questions we strive to answer through our radical rules for schools.

In particular, answers to those questions have to do with the *constraint* (or tension) in the patterns that emerge from the conditions in the system—the conditions for self-organization. When we set conditions in the system, we make choices about how to constrain the containers, the differences, and the exchanges (Figure 7.1).

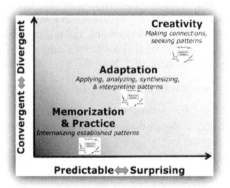

Figure 7.1: Learner's Landscape. This model, modified from the Landscape Diagram in Chapter 3, helps teachers use Adaptive Action to make decisions about what kind of learning experience is appropriate for particular tasks and students.

There are times when a classroom needs to be more constrained or highly organized. For example, activities such as checking attendance, handing out papers, working with sensitive lab equipment all require organized structures, procedures, and expectations. To constrain a system, the teacher might make containers smaller (small groups of students, short time periods, or focused objectives). Or she might focus on a few very clear differences (right/wrong; three choices, pass/fail). Or she might design short, quick exchanges that provide clear feedback, rather than assignments with due dates far in the future.

At other times, when students are engaged in independent exploration or dialogue about a topic, the constraints loosen and the interactions are less controlled. Finally, there are times—like the first moments of the first day of school—when the specific rules are unclear and little is known about this new situation, that the constraints are loosened even more. Recess time has fewer constraints than math class; test situations are more constrained than lunchtime; small groups that meet daily are more highly constrained than large groups that meet once a semester. Leaders who understand the three kinds of change and how to manage constraints in a system work differently to set conditions in each of those situations.

It is critical to remember that constraints emerge from interactions and decisions made *inside* a system; they are not imposed from outside. When constraints feel "imposed" it is important to step back and look at the greater system. This seeming imposition of constraints occurs when rules and regulations originate in a part of a system that is not local. For example, special education rules and regulations feel imposed by state, federal, and sometimes local fiat, and the classroom teacher has to deal with the paperwork, eligibility criteria, and Individual Education Plan requirements. When the teacher's goal is to serve the student, those other constraints may feel cumbersome. The reality is, however, that the rules and regulations are created by the education system to protect the civil rights of any student with a disability, to grant equal access to an education, and to assure those students are being treated equitably across the country. The rules and regulations are structures created by a federal system to dissipate the chaos created when students are not granted equal access under the law. The unfortunate and unintended consequence is the level of paperwork and standardization that has been introduced into the system to manage that chaos similarly in different parts of the country. When teachers and administrators understand these dynamics, they are better able to take the risks to challenge the status quo.

The critical question is whether or not the constraints are appropriate for a particular time in the life of a system. A system's sustainability—its ability to thrive—depends on the appropriateness of the constraints it establishes. A coherent system will detect systemic shifts, interpret those changes, and respond with appropriate constraints. When a system is overly constrained, it is unable to explore and respond (adapt) to changes that may threaten its very existence. A teacher who is unable to shift gears and respond to an individual student's needs in the midst of a lesson plan is overly constrained and less able to support learning across the class. At the same time, when a system is under-constrained, it lacks the managerial functions that enable it to survive. Many new teachers fail to establish organizational expectations for their classrooms and are unable to accomplish anything because of constant disruptions and unpredictability.

At a larger scale, as schools and school districts experience shifting demographics, they have to be able to respond to shifting realities, to sustain their ability to provide effective and productive educational experiences. Developments in technology have shifted how information is generated, gathered, stored, and shared. Schools and school districts that have not been able to adjust to these developments are unable to sustain high levels of performance and learning necessary to prepare students for the realities of living and working in the 21st century.

HSD practitioners stand in inquiry as they consider all these challenges. They expect the unexpected, look for patterns, try to understand the interplay of tension and coherence in these dynamics, and take action to influence patterns toward coherence. In other words, they learn that uncertainty is at the heart of Adaptive Action, and as they take Adaptive Action in the midst of uncertainty, they learn.

Time Out for Reflection
Find a colleague with whom you share a particularly "sticky issue"—a challenge that simply hasn't responded to anything you have tried. One of you tell the story of that issue—how it shows up, what you have tried already, what is still perplexing. Is the problem that the patterns are too constrained or not constrained enough? The other one should listen to the story carefully and take notes about what containers, differences, and exchanges (CDE) work together within the system to generate the challenging patterns. Together, review the CDE list; identify patterns you want to amplify and patterns you want to eliminate or diminish. What actions can you take to increase the C, D, or E constraints, if that's appropriate? What actions can you take to decrease those constraints if that's more appropriate? Rank these options for action from least risky to most risky.

Choose the one that makes sense to try first.

NOW WHAT? ACT WITH COURAGE TO BUILD ADAPTIVE CAPACITY

Once we understand what a complex adaptive system is and how generative learning is, itself, a complex adaptive process that helps us function in a turbulent and unpredictable system, we see the absolute necessity of standing in inquiry, embracing uncertainty, and acting courageously. When we can't be sure of the future, all we can do is search for patterns in the chaos and take what we judge to be the next most responsive step to set the most appropriate conditions for teaching and learning.

Table 7.2 suggests a list of more specific Adaptive Action questions that help us move into an uncertain future.

Adaptive Action for Uncertain Times

What? . . .
- Who are we and what are we about (identity/mission)?
- What are the most critical features of our work (goals/functions)?
- What simple rules (explicit or not) are at work to inform how we function together?
- What are three most important patterns in the current situation? Are they important because they move us forward or are they important because they create barriers?
- Which of those patterns are coherent with our identity and our functions?
- Which are not? What are the contradictions?
- What are recent surprises?

So What? . . .
- So what does all this tell us about whether there is a pattern of curiosity, risk-taking, and courageous action in our district?
- So, as you look toward the future, what is certain?
- So, as you look toward the future, what is not certain?
- So what patterns do you want to continue in the future?
- So what patterns do you want to diminish in the future?
- So what simple rules will shape the patterns you want?
- So what simple rules do we have to eliminate in the system?
- So what options for action will help us generate the patterns we want? Which option is most likely to accomplish what we want with the least use of resources?
- So what do we do, individually and together to carry out the selected action?
- So what will tell us that we have been successful?

Now What? . . .
- Now what do we see in the patterns?
- Now what are your new questions?
- Now what options for action would make the biggest difference in the near future?
- Now what will we do to test the effectiveness of our actions?

Table 7.2: Adaptive Action for uncertain times. Questions that guide Adaptive Action in times of rapid change.

The thing is that educators in general are not known to be risk-takers. We typically do not like to make waves, and we are pretty quiet about our confusions. If we make mistakes, we try to keep them quiet. Our reluctance to share those struggles with one another means that we will miss important opportunities to set conditions for transformation. As educators working toward school transformation, we must take calculated and informed risks, and we must set conditions so others can also take risks. And we must talk with one another about the scary parts. With curiosity, risk-taking, and courage, we can work together to set patterns throughout the system. These quotes from interviews with educators who are learning to do that help us imagine where this simple rule can lead:

And one teacher who's quite feisty at our meetings spoke up. She had a very strong tone and you could tell she really was passionate. But she was alienating a lot of us from the conversation. And so my history with her is to shut down, but I decided I would stand in inquiry. I asked her more about what she meant. So she was able to say her piece. And another teacher was able to say, "Oh, I didn't get it that way. Here is what I meant." . . . . And we realized we weren't even talking about the same thing . . .

—Instructional Coach

Instead of just sitting there and asking, "Why do you think that?", now I ask more high-powered questions. I'm able to scratch the layers off . . . almost like an onion. I just come out with these questions about "Why? Why?" And it's really nice because I'm able to get the whole staff to think more deeply about the issues. . . What I've been doing is trying to get to the core. What is the real serious issue going on so we can actually start to solve it?

—Elementary Principal

What "standing in inquiry" means to me is standing in a position to open my ears and to hear before even trying to formulate some type of a thought about what's going on. It's just being open to everything that's going on, whether it's a negative or a positive situation. And I think that has also helped the other people around me because my reaction isn't a knee-jerk reaction; it's a thoughtful reaction. And so I think others around me are picking up on that. And because they're seeing me do it, they're stepping back and they're trying to get all the pieces before they try and make the whole without all the pieces. So that's what's standing in inquiry means for me.

—District Coordinator

Going through HSD training has led me to be able to (maybe my bosses shouldn't hear this) see failures and see gaps in communication without feeling all the negative emotion—without feeling..."Oh, God, it's because the district cut the budget and I'm losing staff— especially a person who has been so critical!" It's sort of like I can say, "OK, so here's what I see that this person used to do, and there's a real hole here. Wait. Let's stop for a minute. Is this a pattern we want to continue? I mean just because this person did this job forever, do we need to continue to do it that way? Maybe we can think about this differently." And I think having those conversations has been really useful to me because now, when the budget cuts are coming around again, I don't feel that same "Oh my God, what are we going to do?" I just feel like, "OK, there are going to be some things that will have to change and shift, and things will not be what they were, but that doesn't mean some things can't be better and that we're not going to adapt and deal with things that maybe aren't going to be better but are doable for us."

—Secondary Principal

Lately, I haven't been as "nice" . . . I haven't been as quick to say "I totally understand what you're saying." . . . I've been a little bit more honest. . . . I had a meeting the other day, and I said, "You know we're always complaining that we don't have enough time, but we just spent 20 minutes complaining about how we don't have enough time. And we only have 30 minutes left to meet. So is that the best use of our time?

—Middle School Instructional Coach

I think as classroom teachers we're like little cogs in a system. We don't really believe that we have the power to affect the system in the way we think we should. We believe often, erroneously, that we don't have the power to shift the system in the direction we should believe it should grow. And one of my goals is to get people to see that it's not "I," it's "we," it's "us." It's our community, and we have the power to be the difference that makes the difference.

—*Elementary School Teacher*

On our campus, the breakdown happens when the grade level leader is challenged and says, "Oh, I'm not really sure. Let me go ask the principal." The ILT [Leadership Team] decided, "Let's not leave until we all understand this decision and can defend it." So our conversations have been much more open and challenging. We actually are kind of coaching each other on how to answer questions from our grade levels and how to be courageous in those conversations.

—*Elementary School Principal*

These professionals are helping us learn more about what it means to "be curious, embrace uncertainty, and to act with courage" as we work toward generative teaching/learning.

NOW WHAT? USE THESE RESOURCES TO LEARN MORE

Ayers, R. and Ayers, W. (2011). *Teaching the taboo: Courage and imagination in the classroom.* New York: Teachers College Press.

Bak, P. (1996). *How nature works.: The science of self-organized criticality.* NY: Springer-Verlag New York, Inc.

Ball, P. (2012). *Curiosity : How science became interested in everything.* London : Bodley Head.

Center for Courage and Renewal. Retrieved Feb, 2013 from http://www.couragerenewal.org/

Intrator, S. M., Scribner, M, Palmer, P. J., Vander, T. (20). *Teaching with fire: Poetry that sustains the courage to teach.* San Francisco: Jossey-Bass.

Palmer, P. J. (2007). *The courage to teach: Exploring the inner landscape of a teacher's life. 10th Anniversary Edition.* San Francisco: Jossey-Bass.

CHAPTER 8:
Joyful Practice

Simple Rule:
Engage in joyful practice.

Schools, regardless of their bureaucratic trappings, are places where human beings come together to teach and learn. If we don't find joy in those relationships or in our work, we will disengage, and the system will lose its vitality, its relevancy, and its capacity to adapt. Joyful practice is one key to sustaining engagement for everyone in the system. Joy is also the result of this sustained, adaptive work. This chapter offers stories about the essential role of joyful practice in school systems.

Central Challenge	Sustain creative engagement.
Simple Rule	Engage in joyful practice.
Concepts, Methods, and Models	<ul><li>Creativity</li><li>Adaptive Action</li><li>Individual expression</li><li>Game-based learning</li></ul>
Guiding Questions	<ul><li>What is joyful practice?</li><li>When does joyful practice emerge?</li><li>So how does joy sustain creative engagement?</li><li>Now what? Engage in joyful practice to build adaptive capacity.</li><li>Now what? Use these resources to learn more.</li></ul>

Human systems dynamics is truly radical in its insistence on exploring and examining the breadth of human experience in terms of emergent patterns—asking what and how people are behaving, making meaning of those actions, and taking informed action to influence those patterns. Of course HSD speaks to actionable, concrete, observable instances of patterns in human actions, but it does not ignore the less tangible, more personal issues that influence decisions and shape patterns in human systems. HSD is sometimes accused of focusing on the analytical more than the emotional side of human experience, but actually the opposite is true. HSD helps us experience emotions and relationships through patterns. Rather than treating them as separate from and different in kind, HSD helps us notice, interpret the patterns of our emotional experience so that we can understand and shift the conditions of those patterns. We don't have to study emotional intelligence as separate from our behavioral or organizational intelligence—it's all one when you consider the realm of patterns in complex human systems. Toward that end, this final simple rule speaks to setting the conditions for joyful practice. This chapter speaks to that final simple, radical rule for shaping conditions for patterns of generative teaching/learning—patterns that we believe will sustain creative engagement in school reform:

Engage in joyful practice.

We see joyful practice as a path to creative and productive patterns. We can think of joy as the fuel for as well as the product of these radical rules for schools. We believe it is difficult to explain joyful practice because it's such a personal and individual concept and infused throughout our work and play. So, rather than providing suggestions about "how to be joyful," this chapter includes brief responses to each of the guiding questions, along with stories that we believe illustrate how joyful practice leads to and follows from generative teaching/learning.

WHAT IS JOYFUL PRACTICE?

Often, when we talk with educators (and other professionals) about this simple rule, we get significant push back, with people refusing to "tell other people they have to be happy at work." We also get push back from people who believe that emotional issues can be used in manipulative ways to bend the will of an individual or a group. But neither of those issues captures the essence of this simple rule.

We think of joy as a pattern that emerges in a coherent system, where adherence to simple rules allows for the "work" of the system to move forward. Patterns of joy emerge as individuals and groups work together, reducing system tension, increasing adaptive capacity, and finding fitness with each other and with their shared environment. Joyful practice emerges with the release of tension that brings a system into coherence. You can sense this emergent emotional pattern in the voices of professionals throughout this book, voices filled with the energy and joy of discovery.

When Does Joyful Practice Emerge?

This rule invites us to step into a shared space of generative engagement and creativity as we teach and learn. In that playful and generous space, we can be more productive, be open to new ideas, and see old problems from new perspectives. Schlechty argues that, in this space, we can create new mental models about how schools work:

> To break through a mental model that has such a strong grip as the manufacturing model . . . educational leaders must learn to imagine the schools and school systems they lead as if they were organized as places where creativity and critical thought were valued. They must paint pictures that describe what a school might look like if it were a learning organization and how this might contrast with the school as a factory, a warehouse, a prison, or even a hospital. . . They must learn the art of telling stories, and must use this art to paint a vivid description of the organizations they live and work in, as well as the organizations they intend to build. Through such storytelling and the imagery stories convey, the urgency for change and visions of the future are created (2009, p. 214).

We argue that joyful practice should be an essential part of the mental model or mindset of all of us who work in schools. From an HSD perspective, we notice that joyful practice emerges when we follow the simple rules for generative teaching/learning that we recommend in this book. More specifically, we see joyful practice:

- When we engage creatively across difference

- When we engage in Adaptive Action

- When we connect unique individual self-expression to the greater whole.

CREATIVE ENGAGEMENT ACROSS DIFFERENCE

Joyful practice emerges when we engage across difference in productive and generative ways. Every teaching/learning relationship depends on difference. What I know and what I don't know is different from what you know and what you don't know. How I come to the relationship is different from how you come. Our experiences—with both formal and informal learning—are different. And yet, we have all celebrated those experiences when we transcended those differences by contributing what we could, accepting what others offered, and seeing the emergence of new ideas, new perspectives, new applications that moved us forward. That is what we mean by creative engagement, and it is a source of joyful practice. Engagement is also the underlying focus and topic of all of the radical rules for schools and each chapter of this book.

When individuals and groups stand in inquiry to build generative engagements, they move beyond the traditional definitions of "teacher" and "student." Disparate roles of "teaching" and "learning" collapse into new relationships based in generative engagement. Sharing their insights and perspectives, they see, understand, and influence the world they share.

> *For instance, this is the first time, as a teacher, that I have ever been in a learning situation with my superintendent. The fact that we are learning this together and I get to hear her perspective on what this all means helps me understand my role in the district at an even deeper level. And because she is here, really listening to me, I am considering more carefully how I can describe my experience and my learning. In our small group this morning, we all shared new insights about who we are as a district because we really listened to each other from our very different roles in the district. And it was so powerful.*
>
> *—Elementary Teacher*

Adaptive Action as Joyful Practice

Joyful practice emerges from shared, reciprocal engagement in ongoing cycles of Adaptive Action. When teachers and learners at any level of the system bring their own experience and knowledge into the conversation about What?, So what?, and Now what? they contribute to—and benefit from—the productive action that results. At the same time, they set the stage for new questions that ultimately move them into the continued inquiry of the next Adaptive Action cycle. This capacity for productive, authentic action that contributes to system-wide fitness for the whole, the part, and the greater whole is a source of joyful practice.

> *Our principal meetings have changed radically in the time that we have been doing this work, both in the large-group meetings and in our individual conferences between the principal and the supervisor. It feels so much more engaging and authentic because we are using the Adaptive*

*Action cycle to explore what's happening in our buildings.
We started with the test scores and looking at student
performance, but the fact that we can go beyond that to
examine the patterns that contribute to whether students
are learning and then to identify conditions that we can
effect—that makes our conversations so much more
meaningful and fun. I think it's the most I have ever
learned in any supervisory relationship I have ever had.*

—Elementary Principal

Individual Self-Expression to Contribute to the Greater Whole

Joyful practice emerges when we take action in authentic and
meaningful ways to contribute to the system. When any individual or
group in our schools—whether they are teachers, administrators, students,
other staff, community members, or parents—takes responsibility for
setting the conditions for generative teaching/learning, they are leaders.
People bring their own unique questions and expertise, helping to
formulate the conditions, weaving their own indelible design into the
greater patterns that make up the tapestry of the whole.

*I knew that the staff in this department were waiting for
me to prove myself as their "leader." I was new to the
district, new as a director at this level, and returning to
a field I had been out of for the past three years. I knew
that I had been hired to "clean up" a department that
was not well respected and that didn't have a good track
record under the previous leader. And I knew that the
staff members had knowledge and information I would
never get if I worked here for one hundred years because
they had that information from the viewpoint of the
classroom—a perspective I would never have in this
district.*

*So I invited them to engage with me in defining new
approaches and in identifying the patterns we wanted to
generate. Then I asked each of them to choose an area
where they wanted to provide specific leadership beyond
their assigned "jobs." We agreed that they would have
the freedom to pursue that leadership role as they felt
was necessary and that I would be available for
coaching and fully support what they wanted to do—as
long as it was legal, ethical, and within the budget.*

What happened across that year was amazing. Each of the staff members, in their own ways, stepped up and provided powerful leadership in their chosen tasks, which spilled over and created a marked difference in their assigned tasks. At the end of the year, not only did the staff members talk differently about their work, the school staff we served provided strong positive feedback about the changes they saw. I will always believe it was because I let those individuals formulate their questions about their work and pursue their own passions in the fields they had chosen as their life careers.

—*Central Office Administrator*

Take Time for Reflection

Think of a time when you and your colleagues engaged in joyful practice as you worked on a shared problem. Does one of these describe what you experienced? Tell the story. How did it feel? How did your other colleagues and students respond? Would you do it that way again?

- *When we engage creatively across difference*
- *When we engage in Adaptive Action*
- *When we connect unique individual self-expression to the greater whole.*

SO HOW DOES JOY SUSTAIN CREATIVE ENGAGEMENT?

Joyful practice—engaging across differences, taking informed action and expressing yourself creatively—manifests itself in myriad ways. Although it shows up in unique ways because of individual preferences and life experiences, one generalization is self-evident: Joy will sustain engagement in teaching and learning. Human beings tend to continue doing what they find joyful. In our work, we can point to at least four joy-filled ways that teachers and learners sustain generative teaching/learning:

- Engage deeply in the task at hand;
- Connect with creativity, fun, and humor;
- Grant and generate voice; and
- Find creative solutions to old challenges.

Engage Deeply in the Task at Hand

Csikszentmihalyi popularized his theory that people are happiest when they are in a state of *flow*, which he describes *as* deep concentration or absorption with current activity; a condition where people are so involved in an activity that nothing else seems to matter to them (1990). We believe this is an expression of joyful practice, and we can see it among learners of all ages as we engage with new ideas or with each other in inquiry and productivity.

> *If anyone had told me that I would sit still for ten days of learning about these kinds of ideas, I would have told them they were crazy. At first it was just like being flooded with all these new ideas and new language and new challenges. I wasn't sure I would come back for the second session. But I did. And by about Day 5, it all began to click for me. It started to make sense, and I could see what they were talking about. The work I did in my own Adaptive Action started making sense, and I could talk to others at my building about what I was doing. Those last two days in the middle and then the final three days at the end of the training flew by. And I think it was because we were so engaged. We knew that what we were learning was important, and we were intent on figuring out how to use it to make the biggest difference. It was an amazing time that changed how I do my job—it even changed who I am as a wife and mother.*

> *—Secondary Teacher*

Of course, researchers and teachers have long pointed to the importance of play for productive learning and healthy development. Vygotsky (1978) argues that "play creates a zone of proximal development of the child. In play a child always behaves beyond his average age, above his daily behavior; in play it is as though he were a head taller than himself" (p. 102). We think this is also true of youth and adults.

Of course, play is about fun—about joyful engagement with the world and with others, but it is also about making sense of goals, rules, decisions, actions, and consequences. This kind of joyful engagement is currently getting a great deal of attention in schools, especially from game designers and game-based learning advocates. Katie Salen's approach to gaming sounds very much like joyful engagement in Adaptive Action:

We know, for example, that play is iterative as is good learning, and that gaming is a practice rooted in reflection-in-action, which is also a quality of good learning. We know games are more than contexts for the production of fun and deliver just-in-time learning, the development of specialist language, and experimentation with identity and point of view. We know games are procedurally based systems embedded within robust communities of practice. . . Beyond their value as entertainment media, games and game modification are currently key entry points for many young people into productive literacies, social communities, and digitally rich identities. (2008, p. 1-15).

Jane McGonigal is another game designer who argues that games (especially "serious games") have the potential to change the world (2011). Her online game "Super Better" (https://www.superbetter.com/) claims to help players "achieve your health goals — or recover from an illness or injury — by increasing your personal resilience. Resilience means staying curious, optimistic and motivated even in the face of the toughest challenges."

The important thing to remember is that, in games of all kinds—and in generative learning whatever the context—learners engage deeply with the task at hand.

Connect with Creativity, Fun, and Humor

Generative learners also respond to humor and fun. Among a number of authors and researchers, Mary Kay Morrison is another researcher offering evidence that humor is critical to creativity and learning. In 2008, she provided findings about the use of humor to nurture creativity, to increase the capacity for memory retention, to support an optimal learning environment, and to build safe communities that reflect the trust necessary for collaborative learning. Her book served to add to the data that supports what educators know intuitively: real learning is joyful practice, and joyful practice is real learning.

In that first session, when we didn't know each other as well, it was a bit uncomfortable for us to have to work in those small groups to create a way to teach one of the models to the rest of the cohort. I didn't know the others in my group, and I was still pretty unsure about what I was learning....so actually I felt pretty vulnerable in many ways. So when we first formed in the small group, I decided that I was just going to keep my mouth shut and let everyone else do the work. I would help as I could, but my first job would be to hide.

But it didn't turn out that way. One of the instructors stopped by our table and answered some questions and told a couple of funny stories. She sat down with us and used her own experiences to help us understand the model we were supposed to talk about. Then she asked us to consider finding a funny way to teach the model. She invited us to step outside the box and think about some surprising way to talk about this thing we had to teach.

So that afternoon, we only had about 30 minutes, I think, to get to know each other and to figure out how to help other people understand this thing that we weren't sure we understood. And guess what? We did it. We presented our ideas, made people laugh, and thoroughly enjoyed ourselves. And best of all, I will never forget that model we taught—it has become one of my favorites, and I use it all the time.

—Central Office Administrator

In *Gamestorming: A Playbook for Innovators, Rulebreakers, and Changemakers,* Gray, Brown, and Macanufo help leaders understand the power of games to encourage innovation and creativity in organizations. They argue that, in today's fast-changing and competitive world, creativity is essential. Most of us may not think of ourselves as "creative," but these authors say that "successful creative people tend to employ simple strategies and practices to get where they want to go. . . It's like a workshop with a set of tools and strategies for examining things deeply, for exploring new ideas, and for performing experiments and testing hypotheses. to generate new and surprising insights and results (2010, p. xvi). In this book, they explain what a "game" is and how to lead games that set the conditions for creative and innovating thinking and action. Much of the book outlines procedures for specific games that encourage creativity.

Their definition of "game" —and how it is different from other kinds of play—is particularly interesting to us, however, because it is similar to the definition of a complex adaptive system. They say that games have five basic components:

- Game space—where the rules of ordinary life are suspended and replaced with the rules of the game, an alternative world

- Boundaries—in time and space
- Rules for interaction—which players agree to follow
- Artifacts—objects that hold information about the game; used to track progress or to make some aspect of the game concrete
- Goal—so that players know when the game is over (p. 1-2).

The parallel to our discussion of complex systems is obvious. The game space and boundaries are clearly "containers." Rules of interaction show up as "simple rules" about "exchanges" within the system. Artifacts are products of "exchanges." The goal of the game is all about "differences that make a difference." So this definition of "game" suggests that games can be thought of as complex adaptive systems. Playing games can be a way to set the conditions for self-organization or transformation of our thinking and our actions. At the very least, we see games as a useful metaphor for systems thinkers.

Another insight about games and creativity from *Gamestorming* is what the authors call "the evolution of the game world." It refers to the process leaders follow as they set the conditions for the game:

- Imagine the world
- Create the world
- Open the world
- Explore the world
- Close the world. (p. 3)

Although not focused on inquiry and action in the "real" world, we see that these phrases might be a useful way to talk about Adaptive Action in contexts where we need to approach a sticky issue with an open mind and an active imagination.

Time Out for Reflection

Do you agree that learning can and should be like playing in a game? Have you ever set the conditions for learners to make that happen? Have you ever experienced that kind of engagement as a learner? What would be the downside?

Grant and Generate Voice

In Chapter 5, when we explored "generative engagement," we emphasized the critical role of "voice," the condition in which we all feel confident—even powerful—about joining the conversation. Voice is also critical to the emergence of joyful practice. It's also a critical condition for patterns of joyful practice. Engaging with others in ways that allow for full expression of each individual in the group is one path to generative teaching/learning, and contributes to the respect and appreciation that is a part of healthy relationships. It is another indicator of joyful practice.

> *At this school, they really listen to me. On my first day here, I got to sit down with my teacher and map out my plan for learning about Biology. I have always hated school and have never been able to read science books— but I love animals and being outside. My teacher and I talked about what I wanted to study, and I said I wanted to learn about sharks. She said that was fine, and we started working that day. By the end of my time in that class, I had learned everything I was supposed to learn for biology, and I got to do a dissection of a shark as my final test. It took me all day and every once in a while, my teacher would come and ask me questions about sharks, about how they were different from other animals, what made them special, what I had learned about ecology and environments for animals, and how bodies work. Through the day she checked with me, marking off the things I was supposed to learn, answering my questions. When I finished that dissection, I was done with biology. And my teacher showed me how much I learned about something I was already interested in. It was different than anything I had ever experienced in school.*
> —High School Senior in an Alternative School

Find Creative Solutions to Old Challenges

Joyful practice happens when people engage in work that helps them see in new ways and helps them find options for action in the face of their longest running wicked issues. Because they are able to share perspectives and get lost in the work and have their voices count, they are able to apply their new learning in creative and productive ways. That satisfaction in the solution and the excitement of creativity are also patterns of joyful practice.

> *When I came to the district, I realized that there was a long-standing practice that created patterns of discrimination around who did or did not get into the program for gifted students. It was one of those issues where everyone knew it didn't work very well, but no one had been able to figure out what else to do. So they*

*created opportunities to by-pass the procedures when they
could, but basically the procedures still did not work.*

*So we decided to address the challenge head on. We
called together a group that represented all stakeholders
in the system, including students. And we looked at data;
we looked at the law and regulations; and we looked at
other programs. We finally agreed on what we wanted to
have happen, and then found a set of procedures that
would generate that outcome. No one could disagree with
the procedure because everyone had been represented in
the decision-making. When there were glitches in the
implementation, we found solutions as quickly as we
could. And the program today is working for all kids in the
way it's supposed to work. That committee was really
hard work, but it was fun and we all feel pride in what
came of it.*

—Central Office Administrator

NOW WHAT? ENGAGE IN JOYFUL PRACTICE TO BUILD ADAPTIVE CAPACITY

These stories confirm what we believe to be true about joyful
practice, and it is this. We believe that when people engage across
differences in creative ways; take informed, productive action; and
express themselves through their work in unique ways, they are
engaging in joyful practice. And when we see them taking those actions,
we also see general patterns of behavior where people are able to engage
deeply in their work; they have fun at work; they speak up and listen to
each other; and they find creative ways to move forward. We believe
these are patterns that can bring about significant shifts in the interaction
and decision making at all levels of the system. In many instances, these
shifts lead to radical transformation.

When people engage with one another in this way, they set new
standards for creativity and innovation as they support one another in
risk taking and new thinking. They can see beyond the symptoms of
what's wrong to understand the dynamics at play and take informed
action to shift those dynamics. They embrace these transformed patterns
with new-found efficacy and capacity, knowing they created these
changes for the better of their systems. This is what we call joyful
practice.

NOW WHAT? USE THESE RESOURCES TO LEARN MORE

Crowell, S. and Reid-Marr, D. (2013). *Emergent teaching: A path of creativity, significance, and transformation.* Lanham: Rowman & Littlefield Education.

Csikszentmihalyi, M.(1990). *Flow: The psychology of optimal performance.* New York: Harper and Row.

Donaldson, S. I., Csikszentmihalyi, M., and Nakamura, J. (2011). *Applied positive psychology: Improving everyday life, health, schools, work, and society.* New York, NY : Psychology Press, 2011.

Ehrenreich, B. (2007). *Dancing in the streets: A history of collective joy.* New York: Holt Paperbacks.

Gray, D. Brown, S and Macanufo, J. (2010). *Gamestorming: A playbook for innovators, rulebreakers, and changemakers.* Sebastapol. CA: O'Reilly Media Inc.

Hooks, B. (2001). *All about love: New visions.* New York: William Morrow Paperbacks.

Olson, K. (2009). *Wounded by school: Recapturing the joy in learning and standing up to the old school culture.* New York: Teachers College Press.

Palmer, P. J. (2009). *A hidden wholeness: The journey toward an undivided life.* San Francisco: Jossey-Bass.

Morrison, M. K. (2008). *Using humor to maximize learning: The links between positive emotions and education.* Lanham, Md. : Rowman & Littlefield Education.

Salen, K. (2008). *The ecology of games: Connecting youth, games, and learning.* The John D. and Catherine T. MacArthur Foundation Series on Digital Media and Learning. Cambridge, MA: The MIT Press, 2008. vii–ix. doi: 10.1162/dmal.9780262693646.vii

Games and Websites for Generative Learning: A Few Examples

(URLs retrieved January 9, 2013.)

Center for Serious Play
http://www.uwb.edu/csp

Games for Educators
http://www.gamesforeducators.com/

Find the Future: The Game
http://game.nypl.org/#home

Gamestorming
http://www.gogamestorm.com/

Institute of Play
http://www.instituteofplay.org/

Super Better
https://www.superbetter.com/

World Without Oil
http://www.worldwithoutoil.org/

A Concluding Note

We hope that these simple rules can help you build adaptive capacity in your own work and throughout your school system, no matter who you are or what your role:

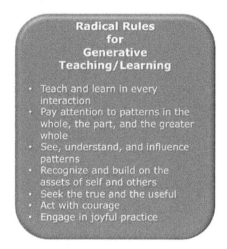

Radical Rules for Generative Teaching/Learning

- Teach and learn in every interaction
- Pay attention to patterns in the whole, the part, and the greater whole
- See, understand, and influence patterns
- Recognize and build on the assets of self and others
- Seek the true and the useful
- Act with courage
- Engage in joyful practice

As we pointed out earlier, these rules are interdependent. They support and enhance one another, but you can begin with one or two—the most practical rules or the ones that make the most sense to you. And then consider the others as your system begins to shift toward the patterns you want to see. Invite your colleagues and students to join the inquiry.

What we have learned as we use these simple rules in schools is that Adaptive Action is the heart of school transformation. As each agent in the school system—from the beginning kindergartner to the president of the school board—begins to ask What?, So What?, and Now What?; as they set conditions for self-organizing patterns, the whole system will begin to shift. With each cycle of Adaptive Action, we have the opportunity to see the emerging patterns, to interpret what they mean for teaching and learning, and to consider our next options for action.

We have also learned that these seven simple rules are particularly generative and can serve to ground our Adaptive Actions, to help us avoid random trial and error in our attempts to make schools more generative and supportive for learners. More specifically, these rules help us address the seven challenging issues that many school reformers have pointed to as central in their approaches to transforming schools:

- Engagement
- Sustainability
- Focus
- Coherence
- Collaboration
- Risk-taking

We invite you to join us as we put these seven simple rules to work in schools. Help us build the kind of adaptive capacity that will invite, support, and sustain generative teaching/learning. That's the kind of radical change that will make a lasting difference in the lives of all our children.

References

Alinsky, S. (1971). *Rules for radicals: A pragmatic primer for realistic radicals*. New York: Random House.

Anderson, G. (2007). *Studying your own school: An educator's guide to practitioner action research*. Thousand Oaks, Calif: Corwin Press.

Ayers, R. and Ayers, W. (2011). *Teaching the taboo: Courage and imagination in the Classroom*. New York: Teachers College Press.

Bakhtin, M. M. (1982). *The dialogic imagination: Four essays*. Austin, TX: The University of Texas Press.

Ball, P. (2011). *Nature's patterns: A tapestry in three parts*. New York: Oxford University Press.

Ball, P. (2012). *Curiosity: How science became interested in everything*. London: Bodley Head.

Barabasi, A. (2002). *Linked: The new science of networks*. Cambridge, MA: Perseus Publications.

Berliner, D. C., and Biddle, B.J. (1995). *The manufactured crisis: Myths, fraud, and the attack on America's public schools*. New York: Perseus Books.

Burns, D. (2007). *Systemic action research: A strategy for whole system change*. Bristol, UK: Policy Press.

Carse, J. P. (1986). *Finite and infinite games*. New York: Ballantine Books.

Center for Courage and Renewal. Retrieved Feb, 2013 from http://www.couragerenewal.org/

Chilcott, L. (Producer), and Guggenheim, D. (Director). (2010). *Waiting for Superman*. United States: Paramount Vantage.

Committee on Increasing High School Students' Engagement and Motivation to Learn, National Research Council. (2003). *Engaging schools*. Washington, D.C.: *National Academies Press*. Retrieved January, 2013 from http://www.nap.edu/catalog/10421.html

Conway, J. *Game of Life*. Retrieved Feb, 2013, from http://www.bitstorm.org/gameoflife/ and http://www.math.com/students/wonders/life/life.html

Csikszentmihalyi, M.(1990). *Flow: The psychology of optimal performance*. New York: Harper and Row.

Davis, B. & Sumara, D. (2007). Complexity science and education: Reconceptualizing the teacher's role in learning. *Interchange, 38*, 1, 53-67.

Deming, W.E., (1986) *Out of the crisis*. Massachusetts Institute of Technology.

Dewey, J. (1938; 1997). *Experience and education*. New York: Simon & Schuster.

Dewey, J., and Bentley, A. F. (1991). *Knowing and the known*. In *John Dewey: The later works, 1925-1953*, edited by Jo Ann Boydston. Volume 16. Carbondale and Edwardsville: Southern Illinois University Press. Originally published as *Knowing and the known* (Boston: Beacon Press, 1949).

Digital Is, National Writing Project. Retrieved Feb, 2013 from http://digitalis.nwp.org/

Doll, W. C., Fleener, M. J., Trueit, D., and St. Julien, J. (2008). *Chaos, complexity, curriculum, and culture: A conversation*. New York: Peter Lang.

Donaldson, S. I., Csikszentmihalyi, M., and Nakamura, J. (2011). *Applied positive psychology: Improving everyday life, health, schools, work, and society*. New York, NY : Psychology Press, 2011.

Dooley, K. (1996). A nominal definition of complex adaptive systems. *The Chaos Network, 8*, 1, 2-3.

Eckert, P., Goldman, S., & Wenger, E. (1993). The school as a community of engaged learners. Palo Alto, CA: *IRL* working paper. Retrieved Feb, 2013 from www.stanford.edu/~eckert/PDF/SasCEL.pdf

Ehrenreich, B. (2007). *Dancing in the streets: A history of collective joy*. New York: Holt Paperbacks.

Elementary and Secondary Education Act (The No Child Left Behind Act of 2001), *Pub L 107-110, 115* Stat 1425, enacted January 8, 2002

Eoyang, G. H. (1997). *Coping with chaos: Seven simple tools*. Cheyenne, Wyoming: Lagumo.

Eoyang, G. H. (2002). *Conditions for self-organizing in human systems*. Doctoral dissertation. Union Institute & University, Cincinnati, Ohio, 2002. (Retrieved 1/15/2013 from http://www.Chaos-Limited.com).

Eoyang, G. H. (2012). Sir Issac's dog: Learning for adaptive capacity. *The F. M. Duffy Reports, 17 (2),* 1-12.

Eoyang, G. H. and Holladay, R. (2004). *Frequently asked questions about tools and patterns of HSD.* Retrieved Feb 19, 2013from http://www.hsdinstitute.org/about-hsd/what-is-hsd/faq-tools-and-patterns-of-hsd.html

Eoyang, G. H. and Holladay, R. (2013). *Adaptive action: Leveraging uncertainty in your organization.* Palo Alto, CA: Stanford University Press.

Erikson, E. H. (1993) [1950]. *Childhood and society.* New York, NY: W. W. Norton & Company. p. 242.

Freire, P. (1970). *Pedagogy of the oppressed.* New York: Continuum.

Freire, P. and Macedo, D. (1998). *Pedagogy of freedom.* Lanham: Rowman & Littlefield Publishers, Inc.

Fullan, M. (2010). *All systems go: The change imperative for whole systems reform.* Thousand Oaks, CA: Corwin Press.

Fullan, M. (2011). *Change leader: Learning to do what matters most.* San Francisco: Jossye-Bass.

Gray, D. Brown, S and Macanufo, J. (2010). *Gamestorming: A playbook for innovators, rulebreakers, and changemakers.* Sebastapol. CA: O'Reilly Media Inc.

Habermas, J. (1984). *The theory of communicative action, Volume 1: Reason and the rationalization of society* (T. McCarthy, Trans.). Boston: Beacon Press.

Habermas, J. (1987). *The theory of communicative action, Volume 2: Lifeworld and system: A critique of functionalist reason* (T. McCarthy, Trans.). Boston: Beacon Press.

Hargreaves, A. and Fink, D. (2006). *Sustainable leadership.* San Francisco: Jossey-Bass.

Hargreaves, A. and Fullan, M. (2012). *Professional capital: Transforming teaching in every school.* New York: Teachers College Press.

Holladay, R. (2000). *An architectural model of organizational development.* Circle Pines, MN: HSD Institute.

Holladay, R. (2003). "Simple rules: Simply elegant!" *PATTERNS, The Newsletter of the Human Systems Dynamics Institute,*1.3.

Holladay, R. (2004). Granting and generating voice in diverse classrooms: Human systems dynamics at work. *English in Texas, 34,* 1, 9-14.

Holladay, R. (2005). Simple rules: Organizational DNA." *OD Practitioner: Journal of the Organization Development Network, 37,* 4, 29-34.

Holladay, R. (2005). *Legacy: Sustainability in a complex system.* Circle Pines, MN: HSD Institute.

Holland, J (1998). *Emergence: From chaos to order.* Cambridge: Perseus Books.

Hooks, B. (2001). *All about love: New visions.* New York: William Morrow Paperbacks.

Hooks, B. (2009). *Teaching critical thinking: Practical wisdom.* New York: Routledge.

Institute for Democracy, Education and Access (IDEA). Retrieved Feb, 2013 from http://idea.gseis.ucla.edu/

Intrator, S. M., Scribner, M, Palmer, P. J., Vander, T. (2003). *Teaching with fire: Poetry that sustains the courage to teach.* San Francisco: Jossey-Bass.

John-Steiner, V., and Mahn, H. (1996). Sociocultural approaches to learning and development: A Vygotskian framework. *Educational Psychologist, 31,* 3/4, 191-206.

Johnson, S. (2001). *Emergence: The connected lives of ants, brains, cities, and software.* New York: Scribner.

Johnston, P. (2004). *Choice words: How language affects children's learning.* Portland, ME: Stenhouse Publishers.

Johnston, P. (2012). *Opening minds: Using language to change lives.* Portland, ME: Stenhouse Publishers.

Jones, B., Valdez, G., Nowakowski, J., and Rasmussen, C. (1994). *Designing learning and technology for educational reform.* Oak Brook, IL: North Central Regional Educational Laboratory.

Jones, R. and Brown, D. (2011). The mentoring relationship as a complex adaptive system: Finding a model for our experience. *Mentoring & Tutoring: Partnership in Learning. 19,* 4, 401-418.

Josić, K. (2012). Complexity and Emergence. No. 2553. From *Engines of our Ingenuity.* Retrieved Feb 19, 2013 from http://www.uh.edu/engines/epi2553.htm

Lantolf, J. (2006). Language emergence: Implications for applied linguistics—A sociocultural perspective. *Applied Linguistics, 27*, 4, 717-728.

Lee, V. E. & Ready, D. D (2007). *Schools within schools: possibilities and pitfalls of high school reform.* New York: Teachers College Press.

Levy, P. (1997). *Collective intelligence: Mankind's emerging world in cyberspace.* New York: Plenum Trade.

Lindfors, J. W. (1999). *Children's inquiry: Using language to make sense of the world.* New York: Teachers College Press.

McGonigal, J. (2011). *Reality is broken: Why games make us better and how they can change the world.* New York: Penguin.

Meadows, D. H. (2008). *Thinking in systems: A primer.* White River Junction, VT.: Chelsea Green Publishers.

Mezirow, J. (2000). *Learning as transformation: Critical perspectives on a theory in progress.* San Francisco: Jossey-Bass.

Morrison, M. K. (2008). *Using humor to maximize learning: The links between positive emotions and education.* Lanham, MD.: Rowman & Littlefield Education.

National Center for Literacy Education (NCLE), *Literacy in learning exchange.* Retrieved Feb, 2013 from http://www.literacyinlearningexchange.org/

Nations, M. (2011) *Generative engagement is about co-creating patterns of authenticity, reciprocity, and justice.* Retrieved February 18, 2013 from http://patternsandpossibilities.squarespace.com/.

Nova. (2007). *Emergence: Q&A with John Holland.* Retrieved Feb 19, 2013 from http://www.pbs.org/wgbh/nova/nature/holland-emergence.html

Olson, E.O. and G. H. Eoyang. (2001). *Facilitating organization change: Lessons from complexity science.* San Francisco: Josses-Bass/Pfeiffer.

Olson, K. (2009). *Wounded by school: Recapturing the joy in learning and standing up to the old school culture.* New York: Teachers College Press.

Palmer, P. J. (2009). *A hidden wholeness: The journey toward an undivided life.* San Francisco: Jossey-Bass.

Palmer, P. J. (2007). *The courage to teach: Exploring the inner landscape of a teacher's life. 10th Anniversary Edition.* San Francisco: Jossey-Bass.

Pappano, L. (2010). *Inside school turnarounds: Urgent hopes, unfolding stories.* Cambridge, MA: Harvard Education Press.

Patterson, L., Wickstrom, C., Roberts, J., Araujo, J., and Hoki, C. (2010). Deciding when to step in and when to back off. *The Tapestry Journal, 2*, 1, 1-18. http://tapestry.usf.edu/journal/v02n01.php

Patterson, L., Baldwin, S., Araujo, J., Shearer, R., and Stewart, M. A. (2010). Look, think, act: Using action research to sustain reform in complex teaching/learning ecologies, *Journal of Inquiry and Action in Education, 3*, 3, 139-157. https://journal.buffalostate.edu/index.php/soe/index

Patterson, L. (2009). When we simply can't agree: Learning to move difficult dialogue forward. *English in Texas, 40*, 3, 13-18.

Pearson, P. D. and Gallagher, M. C. (1983). The instruction of reading comprehension. *Contemporary Educational Psychology, 8,* 317–344.

Pierce, C. M., Carew, J. V., Pierce-Gonzalez and Wills, D. (1977). An experiment in racism: TV commercials. *Education and Urban Society, 10*, 1, 61–87.

Prensky, M. (2005). Engage me or enrage me. What today's learners demand. *Educause Review*, September/October, p. 60-64

The project of the southern poverty law center. Retrieved Feb 2013 from http://www.tolerance.org/

Ravitch, D. (2011). *The death and life of the great American school system : how testing and choice are undermining education.* New York: Basic Books.

Resnick, M. and Silverman, B.(1996) Exploring emergence. Retrieved Feb 2013 from http://www.playfulinvention.com/emergence/contents.html

Rethinking schools. Retrieved Feb, 2013 from http://www.rethinkingschools.org/

Reynolds, C. W. (1987) Flocks, herds, and schools: A distributed behavioral model in computer graphics, *SIGGRAPH '87 Conference Proceedings*, 25-34.

Rose, S. (1997). *Lifelines: Life beyond the gene.* New York: Oxford

University Press.

Rosenblatt, L.M. (1938; 1968). *Literature as exploration.* London: Heinemann.

Rosenblatt, L. M. (1994). *The reader, the text, the poem: The transactional theory of the literary work.* Carbondale: Southern Illinois University Press.

Salen, K. (2008). *The ecology of games: Connecting youth, games, and learning.* The John D. and Catherine T. MacArthur Foundation Series on Digital Media and Learning. Cambridge, MA: The MIT Press, vii–ix. doi: 10.1162/dmal.9780262693646.vii

Schlechty, P. C. (2009). *Leading for learning: How to transform schools into learning organizations.* San Francisco: Jossey-Bass.

Schmoker, M. J. (2011). *Focus: Elevating the essentials to radically improve student learning.* Alexandria, VA: Association for the Supervision and Curriculum Development.

Serendip. *Complexity and emergence.* Retrieved Feb 2013 from http://serendip.brynmawr.edu/complexity/

Simple Rules Foundation. Retrieved Feb 2013 from http://simplerulesfoundation.org/

Smith, F. (1975). *Comprehension and learning: A conceptual framework for teachers.* NEW YORK: Holt, Rinehart and Winston.

Smith, F. (1998). *The book of learning and forgetting.* NEW YORK: Teachers College Press.

Schön, D. A. (1991). *The reflective turn: Case studies in and on educational practice,* NEW YORK: Teachers College Press.

Shor, I. (1992). *Empowering education: Critical teaching for social change.* Chicago: University of Chicago Press.

Short, K.G., *Harste,* J.C., & Burke, C.L. (*1996*). *Creating classrooms for authors and inquirers* (2nd ed.). Portsmouth, NH: Heinemann.

Stacey, R. (2001). *Complex responsive processes in organizations: Learning and knowledge creation.* London: Routledge.

Stritikus, T. T. (2003). The interrelationship of beliefs, context, and learning: The case of a teacher reacting to language policy. *Journal of Language, Identity, and Education, 2,* 1, 29-52.

Sue, D. W.; Capodilupo, C. M.; Torino, G. C.; Bucceri, J. M.; Holder, A. M. B.; Nadal, K. L.; and Esquilin, M.. (2007). Racial microaggressions in everyday life: Implications for clinical practice. *American Psychologist, 62*, 4, 271-286.

Tytel, M. & Holladay, R. (2011). *Simple rules: A radical inquiry into self: Going beyond self-help, discover your ability to change the world and generate self-hope.* Apache Junction, AZ: Gold CaNew Yorkon Press.

Tytel, M. & Holladay, R. (2011). *Radical inquiry journal: A companion tool for simple rules, A radical inquiry into self.* Apache Junction, AZ: Gold CaNew Yorkon Press.

Vella, J. (2007). *On teaching and learning: Putting the principles and practices of dialogue education into action.* San Francisco: Jossey-Bass Publishers.

Vygotsky, L. S. (1978). *Mind in society: the development of higher psychological processes.* Cambridge, MA: Harvard University Press.

Vygotsky, L. S. (1986). *Thought and language.* A. Kozulin (Ed.). Cambridge, MA: MIT Press.

Wells, G. (1999). *Dialogic inquiry: Towards a socio-cultural practice and theory of education.* Cambridge University Press.

Wells, G. (2007). Semiotic mediation, dialogue, and the construction of knowledge. *Human Development, 50,* 244-274.

Wells, G. (2009). Community dialogue: the bridge between individual and society. *Language Arts, 86,* 4, 290.

Wertsch, J. V. (1991). *Voices of the mind: A sociocultural approach to mediated action.* Cambridge, MA: Harvard University Press.

Wickstrom, C., Patterson, L., and Araujo, J. (2011). *Culturally mediated writing instruction for adolescent English language learners.* Final Report Local Site Research Initiative, National Writing Project. Retrieved January, 2013 from http://www.nwp.org/cs/public/print/resource/3621.

Wittrock, M. C. (1992). Generative learning processes of the brain. *Educational Psychologist, 27*(4), 531-541.

Zittrain, J. (2008). *The future of the Internet—And how to stop it.* New Haven, CT: Yale University Press.

Made in the USA
Las Vegas, NV
03 November 2022

58670559R00118